Praise for *Tools for Teaching Conceptual Understanding, Elementary*

This book provides the research and resources educators need to help students take ownership of their learning. It fosters students' curiosity about their environment and it allows them to explore and become life-long learners.

—**Ellen Asregadoo, Fifth-Grade Teacher**
Public School 190
Brooklyn, NY

This book gives a nice overview of how to plan for and implement Concept-Based learning into the elementary classroom. Additionally, it provides practical examples and ideas that any educator can take and implement into his or her classroom immediately.

—**Kate Benson, Fourth-Grade Team Leader**
Colegio Anglo Colombiano
Bogotá, Colombia

The practical strategies and examples supported by manageable theoretical information is exactly what teachers need to begin to take the steps that feel so difficult for many teachers who can't visualize what it would look like in their classrooms.

—**Monique Cadieux, Fifth-Grade Teacher**
Mitchell Woods Public School
Guelph, ON

This is an important book for all teachers. We need to be honoring our students as thinkers who deserve developmentally appropriate intellectual rigor in the classroom. We will not achieve this in our traditional coverage-based classroom. I am so inspired and can't wait to start this journey (making mistakes and learning along the way!).

—**Sarah Gat, Second-Grade Teacher**
École Arbour Vista Public School
Guelph, ON

This is the book that teachers who have been trying to implement Concept-Based teaching and learning have been waiting for. The research-based lesson frameworks create a clear and doable plan for teachers at any grade or content leve   ional coach or curriculum writer.

—**Saundra Mouton, Prir   onal
Baccalaureate Coordinator and   le 5)**
Briarmeadow Charter School, Houston ISD
Houston, TX

Tools for Teaching Conceptual Understanding, Elementary

@juliehstern

Concept-Based Curriculum and Instruction—Series List

Concept-Based Curriculum and Instruction for the Thinking Classroom, 2nd edition—H. Lynn Erickson, Lois A. Lanning, and Rachel French

This resource offers a complete guide to designing curriculum and instruction that moves teaching and learning beyond lower level facts and skills to deep conceptual understanding.

Stirring the Head, Heart, and Soul: Redefining Curriculum, Instruction, and Concept-Based Learning, 3rd edition—H. Lynn Erickson

This book examines the current state of curriculum and instruction and proposes a curricular plan for achieving higher standards without sacrificing intellectual integrity.

Facilitator's Guide to Stirring the Head, Heart, and Soul: Redefining Curriculum, Instruction, and Concept-Based Learning, 3rd edition—H. Lynn Erickson

This guide gives staff developers and workshop leaders the tools to help teachers gain a clear understanding of how to use Concept-Based Instruction to deepen students' understandings and inspire a genuine love of learning.

Transitioning to Concept-Based Curriculum and Instruction: How to Bring Content and Process Together—H. Lynn Erickson and Lois A. Lanning

In this book, teachers will learn how to use the Structure of Process and Structure of Knowledge in designing Concept-Based Curriculum and units. Leaders and coaches will find advice for staff development.

Designing a Concept-Based Curriculum for English Language Arts: Meeting the Common Core With Intellectual Integrity, K–12—Lois A. Lanning

All of the recent research about learning, as well as current standards, mark a shift toward conceptual understanding of complex processes. In this "how-to" book, Lois A. Lanning introduces the Structure of Process as a tool to aid English language arts teachers (and teachers of other process-driven disciplines) in designing high quality Concept-Based units for the classroom.

Concept-Based Mathematics: Teaching for Deep Understanding in Secondary Classrooms —Jennie Wathall

When you teach concepts rather than rote processes, students see math's essential elegance, as well as its practicality—and discover their own natural mathematical abilities. This book is a road map to retooling how you teach math in a deep, clear, and meaningful way—through a conceptual lens—helping students achieve higher order thinking skills.

Tools for Teaching Conceptual Understanding, Elementary: Harnessing Natural Curiosity for Learning That Transfers—Julie Stern with Nathalie Lauriault and Krista Ferraro

This guide provides instructional strategies for use in the elementary classroom. Teachers will learn how to teach metacognitive skills to young students and design lessons for conceptual understanding.

Tools for Teaching Conceptual Understanding, Secondary: Designing Lessons and Assessments for Deep Learning—Julie Stern, Krista Ferraro, and Juliet Mohnkern

This guide provides instructional strategies for use in the secondary classroom. Teachers will learn how to introduce secondary students to conceptual thinking and design lessons across disciplines for conceptual understanding.

Tools for Teaching Conceptual Understanding, Elementary

Harnessing Natural Curiosity for Learning That Transfers

Julie Stern

With Nathalie Lauriault and Krista Ferraro

Foreword by Debbie Silver

CORWIN
A SAGE Publishing Company

A SAGE Publishing Company

FOR INFORMATION:

Corwin
A SAGE Company
2455 Teller Road
Thousand Oaks, California 91320
(800) 233-9936
www.corwin.com

SAGE Publications Ltd.
1 Oliver's Yard
55 City Road
London EC1Y 1SP
United Kingdom

SAGE Publications India Pvt. Ltd.
B 1/I 1 Mohan Cooperative Industrial Area
Mathura Road, New Delhi 110 044
India

SAGE Publications Asia-Pacific Pte. Ltd.
3 Church Street
#10-04 Samsung Hub
Singapore 049483

Acquisitions Editor: Ariel Bartlett
Senior Associate Editor: Desirée A. Bartlett
Editorial Assistant: Kaitlyn Irwin
Production Editor: Amy Schroller
Copy Editor: Cate Huisman
Typesetter: Hurix Systems Pvt. Ltd.
Proofreader: Lawrence W. Baker
Indexer: Amy Murphy
Cover Designer: Scott Van Atta
Marketing Manager: Margaret O'Connor

Printed in the United States of America

ISBN 978-1-5063-7724-7

This book is printed on acid-free paper.

Certified Chain of Custody
Promoting Sustainable Forestry
www.sfiprogram.org
SFI-01268

SFI label applies to text stock

17 18 19 20 21   10 9 8 7 6 5 4 3 2 1

Contents

Foreword

When I began my career as an elementary teacher, I wouldn't say that I understood the importance of conceptual understanding as a teaching tool or as a goal for learning. I tended to teach the way I had been taught, using the lockstep order of beginning each unit by defining key vocabulary words, providing a full explanation of everything I thought they needed to know, summarizing the main principles with class notes, and administering a multiple-choice test to complete the cycle. I did try to infuse my direct instruction with interesting stories and amazing facts and usually ended the unit with an exciting demo or an activity to reinforce what I had already "taught" my students. Just when things started to get invigorating, it was time to close that chapter and move on to the next topic.

Thankfully my teaching methods evolved into much more learner-centered instruction, and what truly changed the course of my teaching was a high school science book by Paul Hewitt, *Conceptual Physics* (1977). Rather than starting with the typical advanced math and complex scientific principles, Hewitt begins each topic with common language and everyday concepts. He illustrates how to present conceptual applications first and then help students use their prior knowledge to develop the underlying math and science principles they need for more meaning. Reading this book, I realized I had been doing a lot of the right things but in completely the wrong order, and I was doing way too much of the "teaching."

Much like the experience authors Julie Stern, Nathalie Lauriault, and Krista Ferraro write about, I began to see that when students are first engaged with enticing central concepts, they are more likely to come to understand the supporting ideas in deeper ways. This premise altered my entire approach to teaching. My instruction evolved from my telling learners everything they needed to know to my guiding them to figure it out for themselves. I began starting my units with thought-provoking activities or scenarios and letting my students "mess about" with the connections they saw. I learned to pay more attention to the naïve ideas students brought with them as well as to develop powerful, inquiry-based tasks that allowed learners to construct their own conclusions.

I have since come to appreciate the value of Concept-Based teaching for all disciplines with every level of student. It is by far one of the greatest tools for helping students transfer their learning to the real world. In my work with educators across the globe I find they usually agree with the premise that Concept-Based Curriculum speaks to the natural way the brain makes connections and seeks patterns. In theory, they like the idea of decontextualizing learning so that students see the connections among what they study across all subject areas as well as their applications to real life. Yet a stumbling block often occurs when teachers face the challenge of planning and executing Concept-Based units, particularly with younger students.

Tools for Teaching Conceptual Understanding, Elementary expertly takes the reader step-by-step through the entire process of effective Concept-Based Instruction for all subject areas from planning to assessment, based on the work of H. Lynn Erickson and Lois Lanning. The authors give educators of elementary students detailed tools and powerful resources for implementing a purposeful curriculum that moves primary learners beyond mere knowledge acquisition to an ability to using knowledge in new and different ways. The authors provide the best possible guide for both novice and veteran educators. They do an exemplary job of demonstrating how to use stem questions, minilessons, scaffolding techniques, and feedback to help students develop deep, conceptual understandings across the curriculum. I wish this book had been available to me when I taught elementary school, and I highly recommend it for those who do now.

Additionally, *Tools for Teaching Conceptual Understanding, Elementary* is true to its subtitle, *Harnessing Natural Curiosity for Learning That Transfers*. Throughout their book the authors express a profound respect for honoring the developmental stages of childhood and consistently remind educators about the importance of tapping into young learners' wonderment while at the same time promoting intellectual rigor. In Chapter 7 they quote John A. Taylor from *Notes on an Unhurried Journey* (1993, p. 45): "When we adults think of children there is a simple truth that we ignore: childhood is not preparation for life; childhood is life."

Their respect for young learners is evident throughout their work. Stern, Lauriault, and Ferraro offer tips for promoting equity, differentiating instruction, supporting social-emotional learning, fostering student agency, and nurturing the learner's passions. Reading *Tools for Teaching Conceptual Understanding, Elementary* is a joyful exploration of proven strategies from veteran educators who value both the nature of young learners and the importance of moving them from surface learning to deeper understanding and on to the transfer of learning to other contexts. They challenge teachers to treat learning as an active, dynamic endeavor that works best when it is shared with students as full collaborative innovators. Their viewpoints reflect the remainder of that John Taylor quote:

> A child isn't getting ready to live; a child is living. No child will miss the zest and joy of living unless these are denied by adults who have convinced themselves that childhood is a period of preparation. How much heartache we would save ourselves if we would recognize children as partners with adults in the process of living, rather than always

viewing them as apprentices. How much we could teach each other; we have the experience and they have the freshness. How full both our lives could be.

Indeed, *Tools for Teaching Conceptual Understanding, Elementary* reminds teachers, administrators, and leaders in education just what schools can and should be. It is a must read for anyone who wants to help both students and teachers to learn and to thrive.

—Debbie Silver, EdD

Acknowledgments

The authors would like to thank all of the researchers and thought leaders who have dedicated their lives to improving the education of young children. We urge readers to advocate for public and private funds in the service of advancing teaching and learning.

Thank you ...

To H. Lynn Erickson and Lois Lanning, for translating research into incredibly practical tools for teachers. Your vision and ability to explain how transfer of learning occurs has been life changing. We hope to have extended your great work in small ways.

To Ariel Bartlett and the team at Corwin, for your patience, advice, and support.

To Matt Connell, deputy head of primary and primary years programme coordinator at the Colegio Anglo Colombiano in Bogotá, Colombia, for your leadership and numerous conversations about how to maximize these ideas with young students.

To the teachers, leaders, and students at the Colegio Anglo Colombiano for your enthusiasm and experimentations with these ideas. Every planning meeting, question, challenge, and classroom observation provided clarity on this work.

To our husbands for your love, support, artwork, and edits.

To our families, especially Gordon and Justine Harris and Michael and Karen Stern, for your support, encouragement, babysitting, proofreading, and edits.

Publisher's Acknowledgments

Corwin gratefully acknowledges the contributions of the following reviewers:

Ellen Asregadoo, Fifth-Grade Teacher
Public School 190
Brooklyn, NY

Kate Benson, Fourth-Grade Team
Leader
Colegio Anglo Colombiano
Bogotá, Colombia

Monique Cadieux, Fifth-Grade Teacher
Mitchell Woods Public School
Guelph, Ontario

Tamara Daugherty, Teacher
Lakeville Elementary
Apopka, FL

Sarah Jean Foster, First-Grade Teacher
Colegio Anglo Colombiano
Bogotá, Colombia

Sarah Gat, Second-Grade Teacher
École Arbour Vista
Guelph, Ontario

Katherine Hearn, Second-Grade Group
Director/Classroom Teacher
Colegio Anglo Colombiano
Bogotá, Colombia

Saundra Mouton, Primary Years
Program International Baccalaureate
Coordinator and Reading Specialist
(PK–Fifth Grade
Briarmeadow Charter School, Houston
ISD
Houston, TX

Lisa Newell, EdD, Principal
Dudley Elementary School
Wirtz, VA

About the Authors

 **Julie Stern** is a teacher trainer and instructional coach, supporting schools in transforming teaching and learning on four continents. She is passionate about helping educators to reimagine school to prepare students to tackle problems we currently do not know how to solve. Julie is a certified trainer in Concept-Based Curriculum and Instruction and served as a specialist for Dr. H. Lynn Erickson's Concept-Based Curriculum and Instruction Certification Institutes. She is a James Madison Constitutional Scholar and taught social studies for many years in the Northeast and her native Louisiana. She is a Verified Master Trainer and has Coaching and Change Management Certificates from the Association for Talent Development (ATD). Julie previously served as the director of public policy and curriculum innovation at the Cesar Chavez Public Charter Schools in Washington, DC, where she led the revision of curriculum in all subject areas for Grades 6 through 12. She has a master's degree in international education from The George Washington University and a bachelor's degree in sociology and psychology from Loyola University New Orleans. She currently resides in Washington, DC, with her husband, a U.S. diplomat, and two young sons.

In 2013, along with Krista Ferraro and Juliet Mohnkern, Julie cofounded Education to Save the World (www.edtosavetheworld.com), an organization with a vision of schooling where learning is organized around real-world problems that require the flexible application of each subject's concepts and skills in order to create a more sustainable, just, and healthy planet. Their summer workshops draw teachers and leaders from around the world to collaborate on ways to transform teaching and learning to meet the demands of the 21st century.

Nathalie Lauriault is a teacher in Ontario, Canada. Having taught for 30 years, she has specialized in teaching young children in mostly bilingual classroom settings. Recently she was awarded a grant for the Teacher Learning Leadership Program from the Ministry of Education to do research on Concept-Based Curriculum and Instruction in her classroom. Previously, she served as the Primary Years Programme Coordinator at the Toronto French School and was very involved with the International Baccalaureate of America as a presenter and consultant. She is certified in Concept-Based Curriculum and Instruction by H. Lynn Erickson. She has a bachelor of science degree from the University of Guelph and a bachelor of education from Queen's University in Canada.

Krista Ferraro is the history department head at Thayer Academy in Braintree, Massachusetts. She is passionate about social justice and civic education. Previously, she served as the deputy director of public policy and curriculum innovation as well as a history teacher at Chavez Schools in Washington, DC, where she repeatedly led her students to winning the DC We the People National Invitational competition on knowledge of the U.S. Constitution. Krista began her career in education as a 2006 Teach for America corps member. She holds a master of arts in teaching from American University and a bachelor's degree in American studies and Spanish from Cornell University.

Introduction

*Why Is Concept-Based Curriculum
Critical for the 21st Century?*

Educators today seem to be faced with a choice: Continue teaching centuries-old ways of organizing the world through traditional disciplines such as mathematics and music, or throw them out in favor of innovation and creativity in order to move into a 21st century paradigm for teaching and learning.

This is a false choice. Here's the important truth: Innovation requires the creative transfer of the fundamental and powerful concepts of the traditional disciplines. We should put real-world challenges in front of students that require them to improvise on what humanity has already discovered. Innovators stand on the shoulders of past scientists and mathematicians in order to innovate. They don't invent without a deep understanding of how the world works.

Innovation occurs when people creatively *transfer* what they learn to complex situations. It relies on abstracting to a conceptual level in order to do it. Although *innovation* is a current buzz word, the imperative to design education in this way stands on a long history of research.

> Innovation requires the creative transfer of the fundamental and powerful concepts of the traditional disciplines.

Decades ago, cognitive psychologist Jerome Bruner (1977) wrote, "Grasping the structure of a subject is understanding it in a way that permits many other things to be related to it meaningfully" (p. 7). He wrote this at a gathering of leading scientists who were tasked with figuring out how to improve schooling in the United States after the Soviets launched Sputnik. These experts wanted schools to produce innovators and concluded that teaching for conceptual understanding was the way to achieve that goal.

Nearly 20 years ago, corporate analyst Teresa Amabile (1998) explained in *Harvard Business Review,* "Within every individual, creativity is a function of three components: expertise, creative-thinking skills, and motivation" (p. 81). Students still need a depth of knowledge and understanding in order to innovate. Amabile's research echoes what Bruner posited decades earlier: It would be unwise to throw out the

1

academic disciplines and replace them with the goal of innovation without the support of a deep knowledge base.

We need knowledge in order to innovate—but facts alone are not sufficient. Academic standards attempt to articulate the knowledge and skills our students need as a foundation to be members of an educated populace. This approach, however, typically lacks a focus on the organizing framework of that knowledge. It needs a conceptual skeleton to give it shape. Disconnected pieces of knowledge are not particularly useful in the era of innovation. Expertise requires that knowledge be organized in the brain in order to be employed to create something new.

> Disconnected pieces of knowledge are not particularly useful in the era of innovation.

In its landmark publication on learning, the National Research Council (Bransford, 2000) explained, "To develop competence in an area of inquiry, students must understand facts and ideas in the context of a conceptual framework" (p. 12). This is what separates experts from novices. A beginner in any field has to work hard to memorize what seem like disparate pieces of information, while an advanced practitioner stores knowledge in associated categories, in something like a giant filing cabinet in the brain. Yet today's standards and curricula are not typically organized in the context of a conceptual framework. And educators rarely make this organization explicit to students.

The revised Bloom's taxonomy—*A Taxonomy for Learning, Teaching and Assessing* (Anderson & Krathwohl, 2001)—asked, "Is mathematics, for example, a discrete body of knowledge to be memorized or an organized, coherent, conceptual system to be understood?" (p. 6). The answer is clearly the latter, but too often we teach mathematics as if it's a list of unrelated operations, a series of steps to be learned and applied with limited understanding.

Nearly 30 years ago, Perkins and Salomon (1988) reported, "[T]ransfer always involves reflective thought in abstracting from one context and seeking connections with others" (p. 26). They pointed to the problem of overly contextualized or "local" knowledge that does not ask students to abstract to broader ideas. "The most artful instructional design will not provoke transfer if the knowledge and skills in question are fundamentally local in character, not really transferable to other contexts in the first place" (p. 28). In other words, we must organize our curriculum around abstract concepts to promote transfer to unfamiliar contexts.

Most recently, the work of education researchers Fisher, Frey, and Hattie (2016) recognized the importance of conceptual thinking in order to transfer learning to complex situations. "As students deepen their learning, we look for them to think in increasingly conceptual ways" (p. 112). Hattie's thorough meta-analysis demonstrates that organizing conceptual knowledge is a particularly powerful strategy with an enormous impact on student learning (Hattie, 2012).

The work cited above only scratches the surface of the research that highlights the importance of developing students' conceptual frameworks. It also only begins to tell the story of how our current approach to teaching and learning largely ignores this critical element. Although most of the research on conceptual understanding does not use the term *Concept-Based Curriculum and Instruction,* it uses identical ideas that pioneers H. Lynn Erickson and Lois Lanning have worked on for decades.

While there are a number of good tools to guide curriculum writing in the name of deep understanding, the work of Erickson and Lanning provides the most detailed explanations, definitions, and tools to guide us toward learning that builds an organizational understanding of the disciplines and allows students to unlock the myriad new situations they will encounter.

This book builds on the foundation provided by Erickson and Lanning and is intended to provide elementary teachers with more detailed tools and resources for the daily activities of the classroom. Readers will find more value in this book if they have already read one of Erickson and Lanning's works and have drafted unit plans using their principles and tools.

> ### Concept-Based series books:
>
> - *Concept-Based Curriculum and Instruction for the Thinking Classroom* (Erickson, Lanning, & French, 2017, 2nd ed.)
> - *Concept-Based Mathematics Teaching for Deep Understanding in Secondary Classrooms* (Wathall, 2016)
> - *Transitioning to Concept-Based Curriculum and Instruction* (Erickson & Lanning, 2014)
> - *Designing a Concept-Based Curriculum for English Language Arts* (Lanning, 2013)
> - *Stirring the Head, Heart, and Soul* (Erickson, 2008, 3rd ed.)

There is a second false dichotomy floating around education circles these days. It is very trendy to emphasize the importance of certain disciplines such as STEM (science, technology, engineering, and mathematics) over the liberal arts. This is an unnecessary choice. The world is interdisciplinary. How can we expect students to solve multifaceted problems like international conflict over scarce resources without deep understanding of concepts such as power, scarcity, and conflict, as well as essential competencies such as analysis of multiple perspectives gained from a liberal arts education? Abstracting to the conceptual level is key for understanding problems and creating solutions that draw on all of the disciplines. And this type of learning is essential for the issues facing this generation of students.

Motivation is another key component for teaching and learning in the era of innovation. Students need to persevere in the face of obstacles and commit to a life of learning. Again, abstracting to the conceptual level of thought helps us achieve this goal. Erickson (2008) noticed a pattern from early childhood education through secondary school: As conceptual understanding decreases and the amount of factual recall increases, student motivation for learning plummets. She explains that when we engage students on a conceptual level, motivation soars because the brain naturally seeks to make connections and discover patterns.

For example, the study of history becomes much more interesting if students try to recognize patterns about freedom, leadership, and conflict. Learning science is more intriguing when looking to figure out how changing one part of a system impacts the other parts. And reading literature takes on new meaning when discovering why authors choose certain literary devices and analyzing their effects on readers.

Erickson and Lanning (2014) explained,

> "Synergistic thinking requires the interaction of factual knowledge and concepts. Synergistic thinking requires a deeper level of mental processing and leads to increased understanding of facts related to concepts, supports personal meaning-making, and increases motivation for learning. It is motivating to use our minds well! (p. 36)

There is a growing debate about the benefits of early academic exposure versus play. We believe that pushing more factual content on young students is misguided, because it is developmentally inappropriate and ignores what we know about how children naturally learn. Forcing young students to learn in a rote manner endangers their natural love of learning. But there is a difference between academic rigor and intellectual rigor. We can and should view all children as thinking beings. We should create ideal environments for them to make sense of the world while being very careful to protect their inherent love of learning.

The use of Concept-Based Curriculum is a way to respect the developmental stages of childhood with intellectual rigor. Infants rapidly develop their understanding of concepts such as hot and cold, happy and sad, in and out. When they are around three years old, they begin their characteristic, persistent questioning. "Why? Why? Why?" By following this natural tendency, we can cultivate their conceptual understanding in a gentle manner that honors their innate curiosity.

For example, preschool students exploring the concept of light in a very unstructured environment filled with flashlights and different materials such as water, mirrors, cellophane, plastic, tin foil, tissue paper, and various fabrics could, through guided, gentle questions posed by the teacher, uncover the conceptual relationship that *the characteristics of the material determine how the light behaves—whether it will shine through it, block it, or reflect it.*

This is a fun, exploratory way to uncover foundational ideas that will build in complexity as the students grow closer to secondary school. The idea is a precursor to many scientific understandings about reflection and refraction of light and even to ideas in physics such as *waves carry energy through different mediums that change the speed and direction the waves travel.*

Kids end up hating school the more it becomes an endeavor in memorization without ever reaching deeper understanding. In *Tools for Teaching Conceptual Understanding, Secondary,* we provide strategies for reversing the ill effects of spending too many years in coverage-style learning. We all know the stereotypical middle-years child who ends up having a negative opinion of learning. This book is designed to prevent that from happening!

Finally, in the era of innovation it is necessary to note that too often, rather than truly reimagining education, schools make small tweaks that wrap up old goals in new practices. For example, we notice that a lot of "innovative" schooling practices emphasize a personalized approach to learning, where students move at their own pace, slowing down where they need more help or practice and speeding up when they are ready to move on, even if their peers are not. This is great practice. But we wonder: What good is personalized learning if the goals of the learning remain stuck in covering facts and skills without reaching a depth of understanding?

Building a Concept-Based Curriculum is a major and perhaps best first step toward transforming school for the 21st century. Education fads come and go. Most arise from good intentions, and many have positive attributes, even if they are not enough on their own. We ourselves are advocates of and trainers for several educational initiatives.

But no other single initiative does more to raise both the intellectual rigor and motivation of students while also honoring the traditional disciplines *and* preparing students to tackle problems they've never seen before. That's the power of Concept-Based Curriculum and Instruction. When we organize our curriculum through fundamental and powerful concepts, our students are able to transfer their understanding to new situations and apply it in unique ways to create something innovative and world changing, becoming the next great innovators.

Chapters Overview

Chapter 1 of this book provides a review of Erickson and Lanning's work to refresh readers' memories and emphasize key points. Specific unit planning steps can be found in this chapter.

Chapter 2 helps teachers set the stage for deep conceptual learning by establishing child-centered, thinking-centered classrooms. Conceptual learning involves deep intellectual work and, if done well, helps students to improve their quality of thought. We share strategies on teaching students explicitly about how to learn conceptually, such as differentiating between a concept and a fact, and how to monitor and improve their thinking during the learning process. We have found it to be an incredible investment of time to teach students the value of this type of learning. When teachers skip this step, they and students can easily become frustrated.

Chapters 3 and 4 are the heart of the book, providing several concrete strategies for introducing concepts and guiding students toward their own formulation of conceptual relationships. Chapter 3 contains important explanations and strategies for helping students uncover conceptual relationships. Chapter 4 provides five distinct lesson frameworks to help guide Concept-Based lesson design. We have provided guiding questions and sample activities, but we hope teachers will use their creativity and experience to breathe life into these lesson frameworks.

Chapter 5 illustrates important principles and related strategies for designing ongoing assessments for conceptual understanding. These assessments are essential for providing information to both teacher and student about progress and insight into what to do next.

Chapter 6 promotes principles and strategies toward creating an equitable classroom through differentiation, challenging low expectations, and other methods. Concept-Based Curriculum naturally lends itself to more equity for students. We want to take this a step further by offering additional strategies. We are passionate about the need to consciously and deliberately work on unraveling the long tradition of inequality of schools. This chapter only scratches the surface, but we hope it will spur reflection and provide tools to aid teachers in this important pursuit.

Chapter 7 is designed to help teachers preserve and protect the innate love of learning that is so natural for young children. We can avoid traditional schooling habits that tend to erode curiosity and risk taking. And we can start experimenting with techniques that foster emotional intelligence and intrinsic motivation. Finally, we explore a few ideas to help students discover their passions.

The conclusion creates a concrete picture of what school could look like if conceptual understanding was at the center of lesson planning. The ultimate goal, for us, is for students to use their learning to make the world a better place. We think this generation of students faces unprecedented challenges, and we need to prepare them to tackle problems we currently don't know how to solve. We feel Concept-Based Curriculum is a key ingredient in that endeavor.

This book is aimed toward teachers of elementary grades who strive to build a Concept-Based classroom. We do not take a stance on a preferred early childhood philosophy, such as Montessori, Reggio-Emilia, et cetera. But we do believe what many of these practices hold dear: Every single child should be regarded as a thinking, feeling, curious, exploring individual. We hope all teachers will find the ideas presented here to be useful, no matter their teaching context.

Recent research demonstrates that even very young children are more cognitively capable than previously believed—and this book provides ideas for helping children develop their conceptual understanding in a gentle way. According to *Eager to Learn,* the National Research Council's report on 2- to 5-year-olds,

> There is strong evidence that children, when they have accumulated substantial knowledge, have the ability to abstract well beyond what is ordinarily observed. Indeed, the striking feature of modern research is that it describes unexpected competencies in young children, key features of which appear to be universal. (Bowman, Donovan, & Burns, 2002, p. 5)

The report also notes that we must attend to individual differences as well as the ages of children when designing learning experiences. As Ken Robinson (2006) aptly put it, "A three-year-old is not half a six-year-old. He's three." We know there is great variance among children in the age group for which this book is designed: from kindergarten to fifth grade. We hope teachers will bring their own understanding of their students when deciding which strategies are appropriate and adapt them to the needs of each student in their classroom contexts.

Many educators have asked for more examples for the younger grades, especially second grade and younger. This book provides tools, ideas, and strategies to guide teachers in creating classrooms that foster deep, conceptual, transferable learning. We sincerely hope you find it useful.

CHAPTER 1

What Are the Essential Elements of Concept-Based Curriculum Design?

Deep learning, big ideas, "Aha!" moments—most educators aim for a level of comprehension that moves beyond simple memorization. We want our students to not only retain what we've taught them, but relate it to other things they encounter, using each new situation to add nuance and sophistication to their thinking. We want to empower them and foster a love of learning. Along with dozens of teachers we know, we have spent countless hours trying to find strategies that build a depth of understanding. But we also know from a mountain of research that the average classroom has remained remarkably unchanged over the past 100 years. The content addressed and level of thinking required continue to largely remain at the surface level (Hattie, 2012; Mehta & Fine, 2015).

Why is there such a considerable gap between aspirations for deep learning and classroom reality? This is the million-dollar question—and we don't want to oversimplify the answer. But we believe that a big factor is a lack of practical, concrete tools for teachers. The methods created by H. Lynn Erickson and Lois Lanning are the most powerful and clear ways to design a curriculum to allow students to transfer their learning to new contexts. This chapter provides a review of their work and is intended to emphasize key points about unit planning before we move into lesson planning and formative assessments. For more in-depth coverage of these topics, we recommend that educators reference the latest book coauthored by Erickson, Lanning, and French, *Concept-Based Curriculum and Instruction for the Thinking Classroom* (2nd edition, 2017).

This chapter will reinforce the following principles of Concept-Based Curriculum design:

- The traditional coverage-based curriculum model, which relies on students "doing something" with factual content, rarely produces deep or transferable learning.

- Concept-Based units focus on using content—topics, facts, and skills—to investigate the relationship among concepts.

- Uncovering the relationship among concepts produces learning that can transfer to new situations and helps students unlock novel problems.

- Planning a Concept-Based unit requires teachers to engage in synergistic thinking—the cognitive interplay between the lower and conceptual levels of thinking—to discern the concepts and conceptual relationships at the heart of the unit; there are no shortcuts.

- Concept-Based planning requires that time and effort be devoted to crafting, revising, and polishing factual, conceptual, and debatable questions.

Knowledge and Understanding

The first important distinction is the one Erickson and Lanning make between traditional, coverage-centered curriculum and one that fosters deeper levels of understanding. What does that mean, exactly, to go beyond surface levels of knowing?

One of the most powerful pieces of research in education is Anderson and Krathwohl's *A Taxonomy for Learning, Teaching, and Assessing* (2001). Nearly every trained educator has some knowledge of Bloom's taxonomy and the hierarchy of different types of thinking—from recall to analysis or synthesis. The first taxonomy was published in the 1950s. Many educators also know that there is a revised Bloom's taxonomy, created by a team led by Lorin Anderson, who worked closely with Bloom on the original version. The revised version made minor changes *to the thinking hierarchy*, such as replacing "knowledge" with "remembering" and replacing "synthesis" with "creating," which it now places at the highest point. See Figure 1.1 for an illustration of the revision.

Most educators are familiar with this shift, which reminds teachers that creating new knowledge is the most demanding cognitive process, while simple recall is the least demanding. Fewer educators, though, have considered the other major change to Bloom's taxonomy: *the knowledge dimension*. Anderson and Krathwohl (2001) have taken "knowledge" out of the cognitive domain and added it as a separate dimension, recognizing four distinct types: factual, conceptual, procedural, and metacognitive.

See the full taxonomy revision in Figure 1.2. Notice that instead of six ways to think about one type of knowledge, there are six ways to think about four distinct types of knowledge. This is key!

FIGURE 1.1   BLOOM'S TAXONOMY REVISION

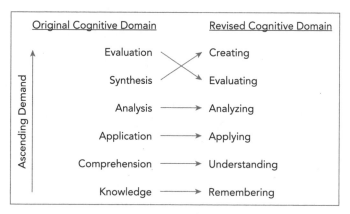

SOURCE: Anderson/Krathwohl/Airasian/Cruikshank/Mayer/Pintrich/Raths/Wittrock, *A Taxonomy for Learning, Teaching, and Assessing: A Revision of Bloom's Taxonomy of Educational Objectives*, Abridged Edition, 1st Ed., ©2001. Reprinted by permission of Pearson Education, Inc., New York, New York.

FIGURE 1.2   ANDERSON AND KRATHWOHL'S (2001) COGNITIVE AND KNOWLEDGE DIMENSIONS

Knowledge Dimension	Cognitive Process Dimension					
	Remember	Understand	Apply	Analyze	Evaluate	Create
Factual Knowledge						
Conceptual Knowledge						
Procedural Knowledge						
Metacognitive Knowledge						

SOURCE: Anderson/Krathwohl/Airasian/Cruikshank/Mayer/Pintrich/Raths/Wittrock, *A Taxonomy for Learning, Teaching, and Assessing: A Revision of Bloom's Taxonomy of Educational Objectives*, Abridged Edition, 1st Ed., ©2001. Reprinted by permission of Pearson Education, Inc., New York, New York.

What is most important for Concept-Based teachers to take away from this revised taxonomy?

- This is further, rigorous research that supports the importance of helping students organize information and make connections between abstract concepts in order to gain more insight into the disciplines. Simply trying to match higher-ordered thinking skills with facts is not going to produce deep learning that transfers.

- Erickson uses slightly different terminology: Facts correspond to knowledge, and concepts correspond to *understanding*. Factual knowledge doesn't transfer, but conceptual understanding does.

- Instructional strategies should match the knowledge type and cognitive process of the learning goal. For instance, if the goal is for students to remember facts, teachers may ask students to use a mnemonic device. But if the goal is to apply concepts, this strategy won't work.

- Assessments should align to the knowledge types and cognitive processes taught. Teachers are bound to get poor results when their instruction is mainly at the remember (factual) level but their assessments demand that students evaluate conceptual ideas.

The new taxonomy is useful in many ways. We love how it reminds teachers to be strategic about both *how* they want students to think (the cognitive dimension) and *what* they want students to think about (the knowledge dimension).

The taxonomy also has its limitations. For instance, it does very little to illuminate the *relationship* among facts, concepts, procedures, and metacognitive awareness. While a hierarchical relationship among cognitive processes is implied, the knowledge dimension does not provide much insight into the nature of each type of knowledge and even gives the false sense that facts, concepts, procedures, and metacognition are completely separate entities. Let's take a look at Erickson's depiction of the Structure of Knowledge, which predates the revised taxonomy. It is simpler than the revised taxonomy and offers greater insight into the *relationship* between factual knowledge and conceptual understanding.

The Structure of Knowledge

FIGURE 1.3   ERICKSON'S STRUCTURE OF KNOWLEDGE

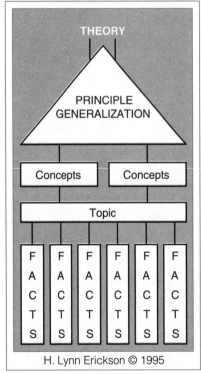

H. Lynn Erickson © 1995

SOURCE: Erickson (2008).

Using a very straightforward and powerful graphic, Erickson shows us how knowledge is structured and provides a visual that helps us to see the *interplay* between factual knowledge and conceptual understanding. Notice the choice of language here. While Anderson and Krathwohl use the term *knowledge* to describe both facts and concepts, Erickson reminds us of the need to distinguish between factual *knowledge* and conceptual *understanding*. The Structure of Knowledge visual also reminds us that conceptual understanding is built by abstracting "up" from factual knowledge or examples to understand the relationship among concepts (principles and generalizations). See Figure 1.3 for her illustration.

Upon reflection, we can easily see how most curriculum design models stop at the topical level. For instance, many curriculum documents list learning goals and activities related to Ancient Greece in social studies, the digestive system in science, or three-dimensional shapes in geometry. Typically, these topics frame a set of facts. Both the topics and facts are locked in time, place, and/or situation. And although they are often paired with a thinking skill—*identify, analyze, evaluate, solve*—they are too specific to allow students to transfer their learning to new situations. When exposed to this type of curriculum, some students are able to abstract to the conceptual level on their own, generalizing about how *communities* work in social studies after studying the class routines and rules, how *systems* work in science after studying rain forests or how *volume* works in mathematics after learning the equation $v = l \times w \times h$, but we should not and cannot leave this to chance.

Some curriculum documents go further up the Structure of Knowledge to the level of concepts: change, pattern, systems. Concepts are mental constructs that are abstract, timeless, and universal (Erickson & Lanning, 2014, p. 33). They transfer to multiple situations. But what allows students to transfer their understanding to new situations is the *relationship* between two or more concepts, known in Erickson's work as *generalizations* or *principles*. To emphasize the importance of this point, we will refer to these as statements of conceptual relationship or, simply, conceptual relationships.

> **What allows students to transfer their understanding to new situations is the *relationship* between two or more concepts.**

The importance of the conceptual relationship level (principles and generalizations) in the Structure of Knowledge cannot be overemphasized. Students must understand two or more concepts and state them *in relation* to one another. If a student can define and identify change or patterns, but not understand them in relation to other universal or disciplinary concepts, the student will still struggle to solve a complex problem involving change or patterns in the future.

Erickson and Lanning (2014) make another important distinction about different types of concepts. Concepts such as change, pattern, and system are extremely broad and can be applied across disciplines—for this reason they are called *macroconcepts*. Many educators hope students will make connections across disciplines, and this is certainly a very worthy goal. At the same time, we want to note that the beauty of Concept-Based learning includes the ability to transfer ideas *within* the disciplines. More disciplinary-specific ideas are called *microconcepts*. We need microconcepts to achieve disciplinary depth (pp. 40–41).

Consider the example of a common early elementary unit, Adding and Subtracting, as shown in Figure 1.4. Think about how the *statements of conceptual relationship* allow students to transfer understanding of addition and subtraction to new situations within the discipline of mathematics. Knowing the definitions of the concepts on their own is not enough.

And consider the example in Figure 1.5 from a typical social studies curriculum. Most curriculum documents will outline the facts and topics to be studied, and it

FIGURE 1.4   CONCEPTUAL RELATIONSHIPS IN MATHEMATICS

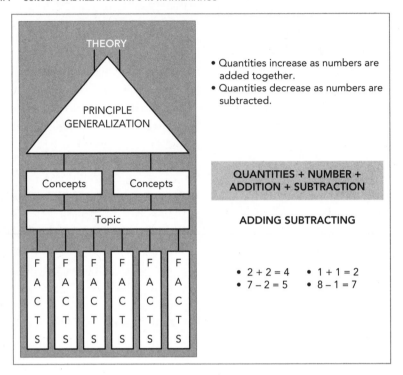

SOURCE: Erickson et al. (2017). *Concept-Based Curriculum and Instruction for the Thinking Classroom* (2nd edition). Thousand Oaks, CA: Corwin.

FIGURE 1.5   CONCEPTUAL RELATIONSHIPS IN SOCIAL STUDIES

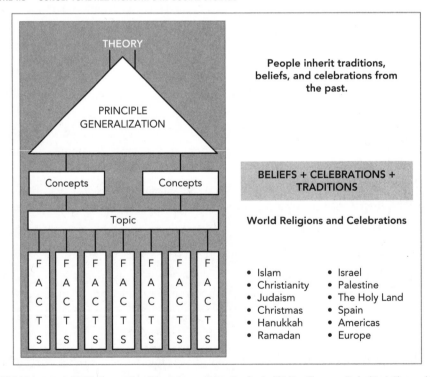

SOURCE: Erickson et al. (2017). *Concept-Based Curriculum and Instruction for the Thinking Classroom* (2nd edition). Thousand Oaks, CA: Corwin.

may be obvious to students that the concepts of beliefs and the past lie at the heart of the situation. But think about the difference between asking questions about concepts (How does the story of "Christmas" relate to celebrations?) and asking questions about the **relationship** between concepts (How does "Christmas" help us understand the larger relationship between **celebrations** and the **past**?). The latter is a much more powerful tool for illuminating meaning that applies across time, place, and situation. Understanding that different beliefs and celebrations are inherited from the past can help students better understand everything from the practices of different religions to the traditions in their own families.

Erickson's Structure of Knowledge and corresponding definitions show us how facts, which are concrete and specific, relate to other key components of a good curriculum: topics, concepts, and conceptual relationships.

The Structure of Process

Dr. Lois A. Lanning is an expert in the field of literacy. She points out that there are differences among the traditional subjects or disciplines taught in schools. Some are more knowledge-based, such as mathematics, science, and social studies, each with its own set of facts that were discovered by experts in the field. Other disciplines are more process-based, focused on processes, strategies, and skills rather than concrete knowledge. In these disciplines, the experts apply a complex process to *produce* an end result. These are language, music, theater, dance, and visual arts.

Teachers of these subjects sometimes try to shoehorn their content into the knowledge-based model, leading them to focus their instruction on the specific characters and plots of stories, the colors and shapes of well-known paintings, or in-depth analysis of famous musical works. These are important elements to any arts curriculum. But the heart of the curriculum is the complex process that the experts in the fields *do*: the writing process, the artistic process.

This relates directly back to the revised Bloom's taxonomy, which separates procedural knowledge from the three other types of knowledge. Anderson and Krathwohl (2001) describe procedural knowledge as "the knowledge of skills, algorithms, techniques, and methods" as well as "knowledge of the criteria used to determine when to use various procedures" (p. 52). This would include the research process in social studies, the scientific method in science, various methods of literary criticism in English language arts, and the steps involved in asserting a geometric proof in mathematics. However, Anderson and Krathwohl do not fully explain what it takes for students to transfer their knowledge of procedures to new situations.

Lanning offers a visual that shows how skills and strategies make up more complex processes, which can be abstracted to statements of conceptual relationship. She explains that understanding conceptual relationships helps students "move from 'doing' to 'understanding' *why* we do what we do" (Erickson & Lanning, 2014, p. 44).

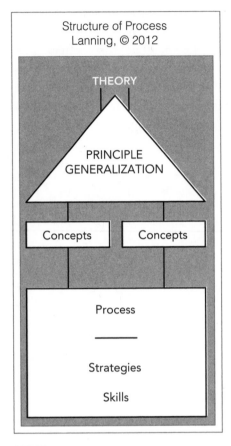

FIGURE 1.6 LANNING'S STRUCTURE OF PROCESS

Structure of Process
Lanning, © 2012

THEORY

PRINCIPLE
GENERALIZATION

Concepts   Concepts

Process

———

Strategies

Skills

SOURCE: Lanning (2013).

For instance, upper elementary students who understand that *writers use specific evidence in order to make their own claims more convincing* are more likely to transfer the strategies and skills associated with persuasive writing to new situations, because they understand *why* this is important and how strong arguments are constructed. For younger students, understanding that *artists choose specific colors to communicate a certain mood* will help them to more consciously interpret and create art to express themselves.

In the same way that Erickson's Structure of Knowledge makes clear the relationship between factual knowledge and conceptual understanding, Lanning's Structure of Process makes clear the relationship between processes and conceptual understanding. See Figure 1.6.

Lanning (2013) notes that, although some disciplines are more process oriented than others, "We should consider both knowledge and processes when designing Concept-Based Curricula," no matter the discipline" (p. 49). Obviously, the balance between knowledge and processes will depend on the nature of the discipline itself. This is why Lanning's work on the Structure of Process is so important. Process is, to varying degrees, an essential component of every discipline.

Synergistic Thinking

So far in this chapter we have emphasized conceptual relationships, as they relate to both knowledge and processes, as the most important components of a good curriculum. While traditional curricula emphasize facts, topics, and isolated skills, we assert that in order to make these types of knowledge meaningful and transferrable, we must push students to engage with the upper levels of the Structure of Knowledge and Structure of Process.

However, we want to emphasize that this does *not* mean that facts, topics, and skills are unimportant. In fact, the dichotomy between teaching facts and skills or teaching big ideas and concepts is a false one. Students must use facts to discover conceptual relationships. And once they do that, they should use additional facts to deepen their conceptual understanding. It is the strategic interplay between the lower level and conceptual levels of thinking that we're aiming for.

Consider the sets of facts and the corresponding concepts in Figure 1.7. Ask yourself: How do the concepts help organize and illuminate the meaning of the facts? How do the facts encourage deeper, more nuanced understanding of the concepts?

> The dichotomy between teaching facts and skills or teaching big ideas and concepts is a false one. Students must use facts to discover conceptual relationships.

FIGURE 1.7   SAMPLE TOPICS, FACTS, AND CONCEPTS

Subject	Topic	Facts/Examples	Concepts
Geometry	Shapes	Triangles Cubes Hexagons	Angles Sides Proportion Similarity
Science	Ecosystems	Pollinators Seeds Sunlight	Living things Reproduction Energy Cycles
Music	Indigenous music	Plains-Pueblo Navajo Zulu	Percussion Rhythm Melody
Health and Physical Fitness	Basketball	Dribbling Layup Jump shot	Offensive versus defensive movement Systems
English Language Arts	Short stories	*Grimm's Fairy Tales* *Rikki-Tikki-Tavi*	Character Plot Text structure
Spanish	Past tense	Specific verb conjugation charts Ir Venir	Time Emphasis Verb aspect
Social studies	Immigration to the United States	Melting pot Statue of Liberty Specific groups of immigrants	Conflict Choice Resource scarcity

Since most curriculum documents emphasize topics and facts, omitting the larger concepts at play, they trap teachers and students in the lower levels of learning. For instance, in a traditional unit on immigration to the United States common in many upper elementary standards (outlined in Figure 1.7), students would likely be expected to memorize terms like *melting pot* and to explain the significance of the Statue of Liberty. They would only be processing information at the factual level.

However, Concept-Based units demand that students process information on the factual level *while also* discerning larger patterns and coming to deeper transferable understandings about conceptual relationships. While studying immigration to the United States, students would recognize patterns about choices, conflict, and resources that would help them unlock other situations of immigration. By emphasizing the relationships among concepts as discovered through facts and examples, teachers can encourage the interaction between the factual and conceptual levels of thinking. This interaction is what Erickson (2008) calls *synergistic thinking,* and it is essential for deep, lasting learning.

Because synergistic thinking is the heart of conceptual learning, it must also be the heart of Concept-Based planning. Teachers, too, must learn to process their content on both the factual and conceptual levels. They must make personal meaning of the content by thinking through conceptual relationships for themselves. This is one of the biggest challenges of conceptual teaching—the intellectual demand is far greater than that of simply plotting out textbook chapters on a calendar. However, synergistic thinking is also what makes teaching for conceptual understanding more personally satisfying and enriching than teaching through a coverage model.

Unit Planning

So how do teachers use all of these insights—the Structure of Knowledge, the Structure of Process—to design Concept-Based units of study for their classrooms? Erickson et al. (2017) offer some useful tools for this process. They note that, although there are many possible ways to write a unit plan, most good plans involve the following elements:

- A unit title
- A conceptual lens, concepts, and subconcepts
- A unit web
- Generalizations that put the concepts into relationships with one another
- Guiding questions
- Critical content and key skills that students will need to master

- Learning experiences and lessons
- Assessments: performance tasks and corresponding scoring guides

In a Concept-Based unit, all the parts work together to form a cohesive whole: Students tackle the guiding questions by investigating the critical content using key skills. For instance, in science class students tackle the question, "What happens when an ecosystem is disturbed?" by investigating a few terrestrial ecosystems—tropical rain forests, deserts, and coniferous forests—using the key skill of testing hypotheses. Through their pursuit of the guiding question, students are looking at ecosystems through the conceptual lens of *interdependence* and employing the additional concepts of *change* and *adaptation*, as well as microconcepts such as *life cycle* and *deforestation*. They ultimately come to understand that *when an ecosystem experiences a disturbance, new conditions enable the success of some species while disadvantaging others*, which they use to predict the impact of an underwater earthquake on an ocean ecosystem.

Erickson and Lanning have identified 11 distinct steps of the Concept-Based unit planning process, as outlined in Figure 1.8.

We want to emphasize one key point about Concept-Based unit planning: It is hard work! The complex interplay among content, questions, concepts, and skills in a Concept-Based unit makes planning tough. Teachers often struggle to write their own statements of conceptual relationship and to craft conceptual questions. Instead of growing frustrated, though, we hope that Concept-Based teachers draw energy from the challenge of synergistic thinking. Think about the unit planning process this way: You are taking yourself on this intellectual journey so you can later play "tour guide" to students traveling along the same intellectual path.

Figure 1.9 shows an example of a completed unit for kindergarten adapted from one created by H. Lynn Erickson to help us think about how we might complete a unit planner. The strands here are divided by discipline or subject area, but that is not to be interpreted as the only way to do it.

FIGURE 1.8   UNIT PLANNING STEPS

Step 1: Create a unit title.
The unit title can be engaging for students but needs to clearly indicate the content focus.

Step 2: Identify the conceptual lens.
The conceptual lens is a concept that provides focus and depth to the study and ensures synergistic thinking.

(Continued)

FIGURE 1.8   (Continued)

Step 3: Identify the unit strands.

Strands will be subject areas for interdisciplinary units. The strands will be major headings, which break the unit title into manageable parts for intradisciplinary units. In a process discipline, the strands are defined: understanding, responding, critiquing, and producing. Strands are placed in a web around the unit title.

Step 4: Web out the unit's topics and concepts under the strands.

After brainstorming, underline the concepts under each strand so they can be easily accessed in the next step.

Step 5: Write the generalizations you expect students to derive from the unit study.

Craft one or two generalizations using the conceptual lens and one or two generalizations for each of the strands. Sometimes a generalization will address one or more strands (especially in a process discipline). A unit of study may have five to nine generalizations depending on the grade level and length.

Step 6: Brainstorm the guiding questions.

Guiding questions facilitate student thinking toward the generalizations. Guiding questions should be coded as to type (factual, conceptual, debatable). Each generalization needs a mixed set of three to five factual and conceptual questions developed during the planning process and two or three provocative questions for the unit as a whole.

Step 7: Identify the critical content.

The critical content is the factual knowledge required for grounding the generalizations, deepening knowledge of the unit topic, and defining what students may need to know about processes/skills.

Step 8: Identify the key skills.

The key skills may be drawn verbatim from academic standards or national curricula. Key skills transfer across applications and are not tied to specific topics until they appear in the learning experiences.

Step 9: Write the common, culminating assessment and scoring guide/rubric.

The culminating assessment reveals students' understanding of an important generalization (or two), their knowledge of critical content, and their mastery of key skills. Develop a scoring guide, or rubric, with specific criteria for evaluating student work on the task.

Step 10: Design suggested learning experiences.

Learning experiences ensure students are prepared for the expectations of the culminating assessment and reflect what students should understand, know, and be able to do by the end of the unit. Learning experiences are meaningful and authentic. Included in this section are suggestions for pacing, other assessments, differentiation strategies, and unit resources.

Step 11: Write the unit overview.

The unit overview is written to read to the students to hook or grab their interest and attention and to introduce them to the study.

SOURCE: © 2017. Erickson, H. L., and Lanning, L.

FIGURE 1.9   A COMPLETED UNIT FOR KINDERGARTEN

Concept-Based Curriculum Unit Template

Grade Level: Kindergarten

Title and Conceptual Lens: Me in My School; Choices

Unit Overview:

Each of us is an individual who is part of the school community. We make choices to meet our needs and wants at home and in school. In this unit we will examine the consequences of our choices.

Standards or national curricula addressed in this unit:

(KCCRS.1) Choices have consequences.

(KCCRS KSL.4) Describe people, places, things, and events and, with prompting and support, provide additional detail.

(KMCSHE.1) The student will comprehend concepts related to health promotion and disease prevention as related to individual and community health.

(K.CC.6) Identify whether the number of objects in one group is greater than, less than, or equal to the number of objects in another group, e.g., by using matching and counting strategies.

(RI.K.7) With prompting and support, describe the relationship between illustrations and the text in which they appear (e.g., what person, place, thing, or idea in the text an illustration depicts).

(W.K.3) Use a combination of drawing, dictating, and writing to narrate a single event or several loosely linked events, tell about the events in the order in which they occurred, and provide a reaction to what happened.

SOURCE: © 2013. Erickson, H. L., and Lanning, L.

(Continued)

FIGURE 1.9 (Continued)

Unit Title_____

Conceptual Lens_____ Grade Level_____

Strand 1

Social Studies
Individual
Community
Choices
Consequences

Strand 2

Health
Germs
Illness
Prevention
Safety

Unit Title

Me in My School

Strand 3

Literacy
Pictures
Words
Details
Communication

Strand 4

Math
Comparison
Greater than
Less than
Equal to

*Add strands as needed

SOURCE:© 2013. Erickson, H. L., and Lanning, L.

Grade Level: Kindergarten Unit Title: Me in My School

Conceptual Lens: Choices

Generalizations	Guiding Questions: F = Factual; C = Conceptual; D = Debatable
• Individuals come together to form a community. • Our choices lead to consequences for ourselves, each other, and our community.	• Who makes up our school community? (F) • What are my roles in the school community? (C) • What is a choice (F)? Why do we have choices (C)? • What are some of the important choices we make in school and at home, and what are the consequences? (F, C, D)
• Germs can cause illness. • We can prevent the spread of germs by making safe choices.	• What are germs? (F) Why do people get sick? (F, C, D) • How can we prevent the spread of germs? (F, C, D) • How do our individual choices impact the health of the community? (C, D)
• Detailed pictures and words help us to communicate our ideas to others.	• Why did author _____ put pictures in the book _____? (C) • Why do people write (C)? • How can we communicate our ideas clearly? (C)
• We can compare numbers as being greater than, less than, or equal to other numbers or quantities.	• How many students are in our class (F)? How many students are in our school (F)? Which group has more (F)? • How can we compare the number of objects in a group? (C)

* Add cells as needed.

(Continued)

FIGURE 1.9 (Continued)

Critical Content and Key Skills

Critical Content by Strands	Key
Strand 1 • Important members of the community such as the principal, classmates, school nurse, etc. • The meaning of choice and consequences.	Describe people, places, things, and events and, with prompting and support, provide additional detail. Role-play to demonstrate understanding of concepts.
Strand 2 • That common germs enter the body primarily through the mouth, eyes, and nose. • That washing hands is an important habit to prevent illness.	With prompting and support, describe the relationship between illustrations and the text in which they appear (e.g., what person, place, thing, or idea in the text an illustration depicts).
Strand 3 • Examples of how details in stories and illustrations show or explain an author's meaning.	Using a combination of drawing, dictating, and writing to narrate a single event or several loosely linked events, tell about the events in the order in which they occurred, and provide a reaction to what happened.
Strand 4 • The meaning of *compare*, *greater than*, *less than*, and *equal to*.	Compare whether the number of objects in one group is greater than, less than, or equal to the number of objects in another group, for example, by using matching and counting strategies

*Some Key Skills may be correlated 1:1 to the Strands (Students will know . . .) in process-driven subjects, but they are less likely to be correlated 1:1 in content-driven subjects like history and science.

SOURCE: © 2013. Erickson, H. L., and Lanning, L.

Unit Title_____

Grade Level_____

Suggested Timeline	Suggested Learning Experience	Assessments	Differentiation	Resources
2 – 3 weeks	Scavenger hunts: The first one should have no details, ensuring that students get mixed up and do not reach the end. Repeat scavenger hunt, adding many more details to enable students to reach the goal. During community circle, ask which scavenger hunt was easier. Why is it important to express yourself clearly? Read the book *David Goes to School* to look at good and bad choices. Ask them what we can do to make good choices at each learning center. Compile their ideas as a list of essential class agreements. Invite school nurse or other medical professional to come in and talk about germs and the importance of hand washing. Compare the number of students to the number of teachers in the school. (More, fewer, or equal?)	Create a big class book, illustrating good choices vs. bad choices and their consequences for their classroom. Create an illustration about the importance of hand washing to place in the school bathrooms. Have a different sign-in every day when students arrive at school. (Example: Did you take the bus or walk to school today?) Children each sign in in the correct column. Students put their labeled popsicle stick in the appropriate jar. During community circle, teacher asks which group is greater or less or the same? The sign-in can be different every day. (Example: Would you rather drive a train or a plane?) Use Intellectual Journal to share what they learned at each center and record good choices they made while working.	Conduct preassessments of the meaning of the words *choices, consequences, symbols, germs, illness, prevention, greater than, less than, and equal to* to find out each student's understanding before planning instruction. Review basic ideas for those who might need it from the preassessment data. Use lots of photographs and illustrations of each of the concepts. Conduct a role-play and ask students to name the choices and the consequences that they see. Then pair students up and give them a scenario to role-play choices and consequences. Place students in heterogeneous groups to explain to each other the concepts of choices and consequences.	Book *David Goes to School* Counting objects to compare Outside guests such as school nurse to explain germs Lots of visuals depicting each of the concepts of the unit

(Continued)

FIGURE 1.9 (Continued)

Culminating Unit Assessment

Unit Title: Me in My School

Grade Level: Kindergarten

What (the unit focus): My choices in my school community.

Why (the generalization(s): In order to understand that our choices lead to consequences for ourselves, each other, and our community.

How (the engaging scenario for students): We are going to invite the preschool students to our classroom to discuss choices and consequences on the playground. We will work together to plan the event. We can draw pictures, use words, role-play, and tell how choices on the playground have consequences for ourselves, each other, and our community. We will use a lot of detail in order to best communicate our explanation.

SOURCE: © 2013. Erickson, H. L., and Lanning, L.

Common Unit Planning Challenges

How do I think of and select concepts for my course?

- Start with the *bottom* of the Structure of Knowledge: topics and facts. Most teachers are given some direction regarding these components of the curriculum. Perhaps your state has content standards that indicate the major topics of study and factual content students should learn. Maybe you are expected to "cover" a certain set of textbook chapters or list of competencies. Begin here. Use the Structure of Knowledge diagram as a graphic organizer, working your way up.

- The concepts should be inherent in the content of your course and the ways of thinking that are important in your field. If you're having trouble "seeing" the concepts in your unit, start by learning more about the topics you need to teach. Keep asking yourself: Why do kids need to learn this? Why are these topics important? What makes these facts or examples significant? What is the "story" here? What are the larger lessons at play?

- It may help to spiral concepts throughout your course. Bring concepts back up during the year to increase the sophistication of students' understanding. Just be sure that the microconcepts and factual content of later units serve to challenge, deepen, and expand upon understandings derived earlier in the year.

- Start big by asking yourself to write one or two sentences that summarize the "story" of each subject or class you teach. What is the one big lesson students should walk away with?

  - Math: We will learn to think deeply about numbers and how they help us to solve problems in our lives.

  - Social Studies: We will explore different roles and responsibilities in our communities.

  - Science: We will learn that all life forms are connected and dependent on each other.

  - English: We will read stories that will help us to understand lives different from our own.

What makes a good statement?

- It needs to be significant. If it feels really obvious or simple, it's not done, unless it's something that students often misunderstand or struggle to grasp.

- It needs to be appropriately challenging.

- It needs to be transferable. We need to think of multiple situations in which it holds true.

How do I make my statements better?

- Make sure the statement contains two or more concepts.
- Make sure it is not a skill or something the students will do. Stick to statements that complete this sentence: "Students will understand THAT . . ."
- Avoid weak verbs: *is, are, have, affect, influence, impact* (Erickson, 2008).
- Ask yourself: Is this a developmentally appropriate yet sophisticated idea?
- Take the time to think deeply about these statements and to refine them. Put them away for a few hours or a few days and then come back. Make them more specific by asking yourself: How? Why? Work on clarity, precision, and accuracy. Pay particular attention to the verbs, making sure they are as active and descriptive as possible. (Erickson, 2008)
- Learn more! This is the trickiest part of planning a Concept-Based unit. But it is also the most rewarding. Rather than take the topics and facts at face value, you must push yourself to understand them deeply. You may need to do some new learning to uncover the deeper meaning inherent in the content. The harder you work on these generalizations, the more you discuss them with colleagues and test them by reading more widely in your field, the more precious and satisfying they become. And rightfully so; you're constructing knowledge!

Examine the sample statements of conceptual relationship in Figure 1.10. For practice, cover up the column marked "Better Statements" and focus only on the side marked "Weak Statements." Use some of the tips and questions here to improve the weak statements. Then challenge yourself: Can you improve upon the "Better Statements"?

FIGURE 1.10   SAMPLE STATEMENTS OF CONCEPTUAL RELATIONSHIP

Weak Statements	Better Statements
Students will understand the persuasive features that advertisers use.	Students will understand that advertisers use persuasive features such as catchy slogans, captivating images, and simple but attractive logos to hook consumers.
Students will understand the relationship between the base-10 numerals and number names.	Students will understand that each digit of a three-digit number represents amounts of hundreds, tens, or ones (CCSS, Grade 2).
Students will understand that there are different kinds of matter.	Students will understand that observable properties help us to describe and classify matter (NGSS, Grade 2).

How many statements of conceptual relationships are ideal per unit?

- A good general number is five to nine statements per unit, depending on the unit length and the grade level (Erickson et al., 2017).

How do I write good questions?

- Strive for a balance of factual and conceptual questions that will ensure adequate engagement with both the lower level and conceptual level of learning. Include debatable questions to increase student interest and motivate thinking.

- Conceptual questions should ask about the nature of the *relationship* between concepts. The following question stems might be helpful in getting started. Remember that the blank spaces should be filled in with *concepts*, not facts or topics!   *◦ What would happen if... ?*

  - What is the relationship between _____ and _____?

  - How does _____ impact _____?

  - What effect do _____ and _____ have on _____?

  - How do the forces of _____ and _____ interact?

- Questions should guide students but not be too leading—this is a tough balance! A question should allow students to come up with the answer on their own through illustrative examples. This means that some of the weak verbs that we try to avoid when crafting generalizations—*is, are, have, affect, influence, impact*—are appropriate for questions, because they leave the question open to many possible answers and approaches. For instance, the question "Why do changes to the environment force living organisms to adapt?" is much less open-ended than the alternative, "How do environmental changes impact the organisms in an ecosystem?" The first question provides a relationship—*changes to the environment force living organisms to adapt*—without demanding that students uncover it for themselves. Don't rob students of the opportunity to think for themselves!

- Questions can make or break a unit, so take the time to brainstorm and then narrow your questions down. For instance, we might begin with the question, "What is the relationship between migration and conflict?" but then refocus the question to allow students to attack just one aspect of this relationship: "Does migration inevitably lead to conflict?" There are pros and cons to both narrow and broad conceptual questions. In this case, the narrower question encourages kids to take a side and reconsider their position at various points in the unit without needing much modeling from the teacher. The larger "What is the relationship . . ." question allows for more variety and expansive thinking, but students would likely need more coaching in how to approach it.

Consider the three sets of sample questions in Figure 1.11. What type of thinking does each question encourage in students? Which questions best guide students toward understanding the relationship between two or more concepts? How do the questions in each set work together to guide students to a larger understanding?

FIGURE 1.11   SAMPLE QUESTIONS

What persuasive features do advertisers use?

How and why do advertisers use persuasive features?

What is the relationship between customers and the persuasive features advertisers use?

What is place value? How do we use it?

How does place value help us to represent large numbers?

What is the relationship between place value and quantity?

What is matter? What are the different kinds of matter?

How can matter be classified?

What is the relationship between temperature and properties of matter?

Clarifying Transfer: The Ultimate Goal of Concept-Based Curriculum

Whenever we ask teachers *why* students need to know what they're teaching, we get a variety of answers. For some, the topics or facts seem important in and of themselves. "Kids *must* read and learn *Charlotte's Web* because it's one of the most significant and well-known literary works in existence," an English teacher may say. But, most often, we hear teachers say that the content they teach should help students lead productive lives in the future. They want students to be strong thinkers, problem solvers, readers, writers, and speakers. They want kids to see the world differently, and to be empowered to act differently, because of what they have learned. It seems that the goal of all learning—not just Concept-Based learning—is transfer.

> The key to understanding transfer is this: Facts and topics do not transfer.

The key to understanding transfer is this: Facts and topics do not transfer. By this we mean that facts and topics cannot be applied directly to a new situation. Whenever we try to apply our insights from one situation to another, we are *always* abstracting to the conceptual level, generalizing from a specific instance to a broader rule, before our knowledge helps us unlock the new situation.

Our brains are wired for this process. A toddler, after tasting peas and broccoli, is hesitant to try spinach; he has created a generalization that relates taste and color to help guide his decisions when faced with a new vegetable. Another child predicts that the princess will be rescued from the clutches of the evil queen after watching several Disney movies where "good triumphs over evil." We move naturally between factual instances and the conceptual rules or patterns that make up the logic of our world.

The problem is, if we remain at the topic and factual level, students stop trying to derive larger principles about what they're learning. By the time they reach upper elementary school, they have been conditioned to retrieve knowledge on cue without deep understanding. But we continue to expect transfer. Knowing that students read *Charlie and the Chocolate Factory* last year, we assume they will have more insight into *James and the Giant Peach*. Once they've learned to perform calculations involving fractions, we expect them to solve a word problem that asks them to cut a recipe in half or to double it. We're surprised when learning doesn't transfer in these ways. Too often, we assign students a poor grade and move on.

The great thing about conceptual learning is that it makes visible and concrete the process by which we turn our knowledge of facts into transferable, conceptual understandings. If students use their reading of *Charlie and the Chocolate Factory* to investigate the relationship between the concepts of fate and free will, spending considerable time refining their generalizations about these concepts, they will more readily recognize their generalizations at work when they read *James and the Giant Peach*. And when young math students use their study of fractions to investigate the relationship between multiplication and division, rather than just memorizing the algorithms, they are more capable of attacking a tough word problem where the appropriate algorithm is not obvious.

These are examples of *academic transfer*, meaning the transfer of understanding from one school assignment to the next. When we talk about transfer of learning in this book, we are also talking about *transfer to real-world situations or problems*. This means that students' understanding of conceptual relationships should alter how they see the world *beyond* the walls of the classroom and how they solve problems that occur outside the neat, teacher-constructed parameters of an academic exercise. For us, the ultimate goal is not just to transfer understanding from the study of *Charlie and the Chocolate Factory* to the study of *James and the Giant Peach*. It's great for students to understand how views of free will and fate impact the characters of these stories, but it's even better when they can apply these insights to solving, say, conflicts in school by recognizing that students' decisions to stand up against bullying are related to the degree to which they see themselves as in control of situations.

Notice that *conceptual transfer* is different from *making connections*. Teachers often ask students to make topical or factual connections to extend learning and make it meaningful. For instance, when her class is studying the impact of germs on the body, a health teacher may ask students to read articles about the problem of lack of proper hand washing in the spread of infection and decide whether or not they would support a law that required all children to wash their hands before eating snack or lunch. Clearly, students must draw on what they know to respond to this assignment. But they are not asked to draw on *concepts*; rather, they are asked

> Conceptual transfer only occurs when students apply insights about the relationship among concepts to a new scenario.

to rely on facts about the topic of germs. Conceptual transfer only occurs when students apply insights about the relationship among concepts to a new scenario.

Educational researcher John Hattie's work supports the claim that conceptual understanding is key to transferring learning to new situations. He explained,

> We come to know ideas, and then we can be asked to relate and extend them. This leads to conceptual understanding, which can in turn become a new idea—and so the cycle continues. These conceptual understandings form the "coat hangers" on which we interpret and assimilate new ideas, and relate and extend them. (Hattie, 2012, p. 115)

FIGURE 1.12   SURFACE, DEEP, AND TRANSFER LEARNING

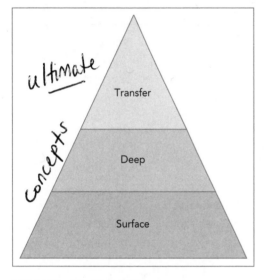

SOURCE: Fisher, Frey, & Hattie (2016).

He says there are three distinct levels of learning: surface, deep, and transfer. See Figure 1.12. All three levels are essential, and you will see us reiterate that point in the section on what Erickson calls "synergistic thinking." Hattie and his coauthors stated, "Together, surface and deep understanding lead to the student developing conceptual understanding" (p. 61). They agree that "the ultimate goal, and one that is hard to realize, is transfer. When students reach this level, learning has been accomplished" (Fisher, Frey, & Hattie, 2016, p. 19).

In the 1980s, researchers Perkins and Salomon (1988) coined a distinction between what they called *low-road* transfer and *high-road* transfer. Essentially, when tasks remain similar to one another, this is known as low-road transfer. When students are asked to transfer knowledge to dissimilar tasks, which requires them to increasingly generalize concepts, they are performing high-road transfer.

For those who agree that the 21st century demands innovation, this thinking by the titans in educational research cannot be ignored. Innovation is high-road, real-world transfer of learning. And it is done at the conceptual level.

> Innovation is high-road, real-world transfer of learning. And it is done at the conceptual level.

We've combined Perkins and Salomon's high-road and low-road transfer with our academic and real-world transfer to illustrate the key to fostering innovation, as shown in Figure 1.13. Formal schooling needs to live in all four quadrants of this figure, because a deep foundation of facts or surface-level learning is key for deep learning, transfer, and innovation. But the point is that the upper right quadrant is where innovation happens. And this book will show you how to reach this point.

For example, young students studying communities might explore the relationship between *communities* and *rules*. The teacher could pose a question such as, "Why do communities create rules?" She could start with a context of the classroom, asking students to explore the rules and the reasons behind them. They would likely conclude something like, "Communities create rules to help everyone get along." To deepen their understanding, they could explore the larger school community and rules beyond the literal classroom walls.

FIGURE 1.13   WHERE INNOVATION HAPPENS

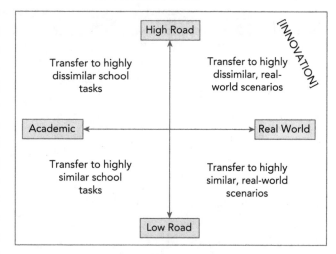

SOURCE: Stern, Ferraro, & Mohnkern (2016).

Next, she could ask them about their families, where they can explore examples of family rules and how those rules help everyone to get along.

Notice how each context moves students from the lower left quadrant of Figure 1.13 toward the upper right quadrant. As a summative task, students could tackle the problem of accidents at an ice-skating rink. They could propose rules that might help everyone to get along. One group of students might suggest making the first half hour of every hour for beginners, while the second half hour is reserved for experienced skaters wanting to go faster. Another group could suggest placing a rope around the middle of the rink where beginners could practice safely while experienced skaters use the outer part of the rink to go faster. When we abstract to the conceptual level and transfer understanding to increasingly complex tasks, young children can practice real-world, innovative problem solving!

Figure 1.14 on the following page shows how upper elementary students can work toward solving an incredibly complex problem. It was designed in a graduate class at the University of North Carolina at Wilmington by Professor Elizabeth Crawford and some of her students. The questions are labeled as factual (f) or conceptual (c). You can find the entire unit along with excellent resources at http://climatelets makeachange.weebly.com/.

Climate: Let's Make a Change!

By Lauren Breen, Elizabeth Crawford, John Clark, and Meredith Mitchell

In *Climate: Let's Make a Change!* upper-elementary-grade students learn about the root causes and impacts of climate change on humans, other living beings, and ecosystems. Students will uncover and refine their conceptual understandings of conservation, cause and effect, change, interdependence, sustainability, and systems through visible thinking routines; written and oral responses to texts, film, and photographs; and

Lesson	Conceptual Relationship	Guiding Questions
Lesson 1 3-2-1 Climate Change!	Human activities accelerate changes to Earth's climate system.	• How do human activities impact Earth's climate system? (c) • How can humans change behaviors in order to live more sustainably? (c) • What are the indicators of environmental change? (f) • What lifestyle choices have the most/least significant impact on ecological footprint? (f)
Lesson 2 Polar Bears, Farms, Climate Change, Oh My!	Climate change disrupts the ecological balance between interdependent plant and animal species and diminishes ecological biodiversity necessary for survival.	• How do global temperature changes impact ecological systems? (c) • How do changes within and between ecosystems impact plant and animal survival? (c) • How do changes in CO_2 impact plant and animal species within an ecosystem? (f) • How do changes in the world's oceans (e.g., sea level, acidity, temperature) impact life on Earth? (f) • How does climate change contribute to the spread of disease? (f)
Lesson 3 Food for Thought	Human dietary choices contribute to climate change.	• How do consumer choices impact climate systems and ecological systems? (c) • What factors contribute to food's impact on climate? (f) • Which dietary choices have the most and least impact on climate change? (f)
Lesson 4 We're Going Off the Grid!	Plant and animal species' survival necessitates adaptation to ecological changes.	• How do humans adapt to and mitigate climate change? (c) • What structural and behavioral adaptations do species undergo to ensure their survival? (c) • What daily lifestyle changes can lower humans' ecological footprints and, thus, their impacts on climate change? (f)
Lesson 5 Climate: Let's Make a Change!	Social interactions impact individual and group lifestyle choices.	• How do social interactions influence individual and group lifestyle choices? (c) • What are effective individual and collective actions to mitigate future climate change? (f) • How can activism promote environmental sustainability? (f)

SOURCE: Lauren Breen, Elizabeth Crawford, John Clark, and Meredith Mitchell, University of North Carolina at Wilmington.

comparing and contrasting examples, among other authentic activities that explore the conceptual relationships in different contexts. Students will recognize that climate impacts all life on earth. The unit's culminating project engages students in creating solutions to reduce their ecological footprint. See Figure 1.14 for a breakdown of each lesson along with a conceptual relationship and corresponding guiding questions.

Conclusion

We hope that this chapter was a helpful review of the most important principles of Concept-Based Curriculum and of the basic steps for planning a Concept-Based unit. What excites us most about this curriculum model is its ability to awaken the potential of young people as intellectuals and as solvers of complex problems. When we envision the type of education that moves beyond rote learning, and instead treats students as capable contributors to our global community, Concept-Based is at the heart of it. This is because conceptual learning focuses on transferring deep, lasting insights to novel situations instead of "covering" a pile of information or set of discrete learning objectives. It encourages students to uncover meaningful truths and make use of them instead of cramming for tests that have no value beyond the schoolhouse walls.

By no means has this been a comprehensive guide. If you're left yearning for more in-depth explanations and further examples, we recommend that teachers of language (including world or foreign languages) and arts (music, drama, etc.) read Lanning's *Designing a Concept-Based Curriculum for English Language Arts: Meeting the Common Core With Intellectual Integrity* (2013). Everyone else should check out Erickson, Lanning, and French's *Concept-Based Curriculum and Instruction for the Thinking Classroom* (2nd edition, 2017).

Chapter Review

- What role do facts, topics, and concepts play in a Concept-Based Curriculum? What about skills, strategies, processes, and concepts? Why are all of these elements important?

- What does it mean to make *transfer* the goal of learning? Why are concepts essential to the transfer of understanding from one situation to another?

- What are the greatest challenges of planning a Concept-Based unit? Which insights from this chapter might help you get "unstuck" during the tough parts of your planning process?

....

CHAPTER 2

How Do I Set Up My Classroom for Deep, Conceptual Learning?

In this chapter, we outline the building blocks of a Concept-Based classroom and offer strategies to help elementary teachers establish a culture conducive to building students' conceptual understanding. Concept-Based teachers operate from four basic principles when setting up their classroom dynamics:

1. We can **honor** developmental stages of **childhood** with intellectual rigor.

2. Conceptual learning happens best in a student-centered, **thinking-centered** classroom.

3. It is important to **teach students explicitly** about how to learn conceptually.

4. Conceptual learning is **iterative**; students need chances to refine and increase the sophistication of their thinking.

This chapter offers a brief explanation of each of these principles and several illustrative instructional strategies to get you thinking—and teaching—like a Concept-Based teacher.

Honoring Childhood With Intellectual Rigor

We wholeheartedly believe that kids of all ages are able to handle more intellectual rigor than most teachers give them. This does not mean more facts for them to memorize or teaching at a faster pace. It means that they, even at a very young age, can usually make more connections, draw more conclusions, and hypothesize more potential solutions than we typically ask them to do. Of course, there is a range of developmental appropriateness; we are not going to ask a 5-year-old to drive a car or read Plato. But we can engage them on an intellectual level by asking the questions listed in Chapter 1, such as how two things are related, how something affects something else, why something happens, and more "what if" types of questions.

As stated in the introduction, an overwhelming amount of recent evidence demonstrates that babies and preschoolers are capable of more complex thought than was previously believed—and that a stimulating, nurturing environment from a young age can literally change the physiological makeup of the brain (Bowman, Donovan, & Burns, 2002). The trick is figuring out the ideal amount of stimulation—it's like Goldilocks: not too much, not too little, but just right. And it can vary greatly from kid to kid, no matter the age.

Based on a mountain of research (Bowman et al., 2002; Hattie, 2009; to name a few) the keys to honoring childhood with intellectual rigor are as follows:

- Have a set of specific, written **learning goals** that you want students to master.
- Plan and **prepare** students for successful explorations.
- Give lots of opportunity for exploration and child-directed **discovery (**or what we call **un-coverage)** of those goals.
- Allow significant time for **reflection** and **questions** that probe thinking and metacognition.

Chapter 3 will go into more details about exactly how to facilitate student discovery or un-coverage of your conceptual learning goals. For now, let's focus on specific ways to set up your classroom dynamics.

Strategy #1: Set up a space ripe for exploration.

Elementary teachers are skillful at brainstorming materials that will engage student interest and help them to discover how the world works. We encourage teachers to constantly think about the materials that will best support the un-coverage of learning goals. It can be helpful to organize and categorize things by concepts, such as using a large box labeled "motion, energy, and force" with a set of magnets, ramps, cars, balls of different sizes, feathers, weights, a spinning top toy, a Newton's cradle toy, and laminated images of things such as kids swinging, kids sledding down a hill, a cheetah running, et cetera. We like to put concepts into Google to kick-start our thinking about materials. Google Images offers many ideas that can be printed and laminated to help students visualize the concepts. Figure 2.1 contains a list of ideas meant to help you get started—of course there is a lot of overlap, and materials can be used for many different explorations. For example, a balance scale can be used to explore both math and science concepts and social studies, because it is the classic symbol for justice.

FIGURE 2.1 EXAMPLES OF SUPPLIES IN A CONCEPT-BASED CLASSROOM

Idea	Description
Reflection Wall	Draw or print an image of a child with a giant thought bubble coming from his head. Put an example of a reflection related to your learning goal such as, "I notice that when I throw a heavier ball at the foam, it causes more damage than when I throw a lighter ball. That makes me think that the heavier the object, the greater the force it carries when thrown, and therefore the greater the impact when it collides with another object."
Question Box	Put a set of question stems or questions related to the learning goal in a box, and regularly have students select one to answer about their exploration. See Figures 2.2 and 2.4 for question stems and ideas.
Science Materials	Blocks, magnets, cars, ramps, balls, flashlights, mirrors, sandpaper, tissue paper, cellophane, tin foil, sponges, clay, baking soda, vinegar, flour, water, plants and plant materials, images or replicas of different inherited traits, models of different systems such as the skeletal system or solar system, models or mini versions of different habitats or ecosystems—can include classroom pets, images of local wildlife, remote controlled toys, compost area
Social Studies Materials	Make-believe area and supplies (e.g. play kitchen, costumes), topographical maps and models, globes, flags, compass/GPS, play money, items from different world religions and cultures, art and iconic cultural replicas, historical texts, recycle station, newspapers, news magazines, books about different cultures and places
Art Materials	Crayons, markers, glitter pens, glue, rubber cement, child-safe scissors, play dough, paint, chalk, recycled materials, music, musical instruments, puppets, different fabrics
Math Materials	Numerous items for counting such as little bears, counting chips, counting bead strings, dice, dot patterns on cards, number lines, bar graphs, scales, geometric shapes, data charts
Language Materials	Books, letter stickers, magnet letters, letters and words to color, magazines filled with images to explore and cut out, boxes of objects that all start with the same letter, poems, songs

Strategy #2: Establish an environment with *questions* as key tools for learning.

As students explore, it is essential to use questions at key points along the way. Figure 2.2 has a list of question stems along with related sample questions. You might say something like,

In this classroom we are explorers! Our goal is to discover how the world works and have fun while we do it. One of our main tools as explorers is questions. We will ask and answer lots and lots and lots of questions. As your teacher I will start by asking each of you a series of questions. Over here is our question wall. Every day we will ask and answer questions such as . . . [see Figure 2.2]. Let's practice by answering some of these questions.

FIGURE 2.2   SAMPLE QUESTION STEMS

Question Stems	Sample Questions
What do we know about . . . ? What is its purpose?	What do we know about numbers? What are they? Why do we have them?
When we did (something) . . ., why did (another thing) . . . happen?	When we built the tower really tall, why did it fall down?
How does . . . ?	How does water affect plants?
What might happen if we . . . ?	What might happen if we didn't have any rules in our community?

Next, interview each student and take notes of their interests and what they think about key concepts and ideas related to your learning goals. This will demonstrate the important role of questions in a one-on-one setting and give you great insight into each child's thinking.

Early Elementary: Early childhood philosophies that emphasize the importance of play and student-centered classrooms are gaining more popularity. This is different, though, from a completely unstructured environment that is more akin to daycare than preschool. The balance we need to strike is having a set of goals and providing opportunities for students to reach those goals without being overly rigid or adult directed. A danger we often see is when teachers do things *for* children in the hope of showing some sort of end product of their learning. A funny anecdote: I asked my two-year-old—who gave me a pretty painting for Mother's Day that had his footprints as flowers—who had made his painting, and he said matter-of-factly, "Miss Marta" (his teacher). Of course, we are not talking about two-year-olds and Mother's Day paintings but still, we need to be careful that we are not too invasive in their learning journey.

One of the major sticking points of Concept-Based Curriculum and Instruction is that teachers articulate and craft learning goals of conceptual relationship for students. We encourage play-based learning and following student interests as methods to uncover conceptual understandings. But we want to be clear that it requires gentle guidance and prompting from adults for students to develop the organizing ideas essential for building expertise.

For example, imagine a classroom where kindergarten students showed an interest in ramps. The teacher noticed that their interest increased and added new elements to their play supplies, such as ways to make the ramps taller and longer and different materials to use to make the ramps. By the end of the lesson, students had formed their own definition of *ramp*. We support the idea that teachers followed student interest. We would simply suggest that the teachers take it one step further by asking students to notice the difference in the speed of cars or balls going down the ramp based on the steepness of the ramp. Students could uncover the idea that *the steepness of the ramp determines the speed an object will travel. The steeper the ramp, the faster the ball or car will go.*

It can be difficult to find the right balance between child-guided and adult-guided learning experiences. We like Anne Epstein's stance in *The Intentional Teacher* (2014) published by the National Association for the Education of Young Children: "Both young children and teachers have active roles in the learning process" (p. xii). She cites a tremendous amount of research to support her position and includes, "Rarely does learning come about entirely through a child's efforts or only from adult instruction" (p. 2). Figure 2.3 shows the guidelines she offers for deciding when learning through child-guided exploration is best and when adults should consider more guidance.

FIGURE 2.3   GUIDELINES FOR CHILD- AND ADULT-GUIDED LEARNING

Support child-guided learning when children are	Employ adult-guided learning when children
• Exploring materials, actions, and ideas actively and making connections on their own.	• Have not yet encountered the material or experience at home or in other settings.
• Establishing interpersonal relationships and learnings from one another.	• Cannot create established systems of knowledge (such as letter names) on their own.
• Turning to one another for assistance.	• Do not see, hear, or otherwise attend to something likely to interest them.
• Considering and investigating their own questions about materials, events, and ideas.	• Have not reflected on how or why something has happened, or considered what might happen "if . . . ."
• Motivated to solve a problem on their own.	• Do not engage with something teachers know they will need for further learning.
• So focused on their enterprise that adult intervention would be an interruption.	

(Continued)

FIGURE 2.3   (Continued)

• Challenging themselves and one another to master new skills. • Applying and extending existing knowledge and skills in new ways.	• Ask for information or help explicitly. • Are bored or distracted and need help focusing. • Appear stalled, discouraged, or frustrated. • Appear ready for the next level of mastery but are not likely to attain it on their own. • Are not aware of the potentially unsafe or hurtful consequences of their actions. • Appear to use materials or actions very repetitively over time. • Are conscious of and upset about something they cannot yet do but wish to.

Although some strategies in this book are clearly for older students who can read and write, we place ideas throughout the chapters for early elementary or those who cannot read and write very well yet. It is also extremely important to keep in mind that individual children can vary greatly in what they are ready to take on, no matter the age. Therefore, we hope teachers will get to know their students well, and try out, modify, and use the different strategies in different ways with their students.

Setting the Foundation for a Thinking Classroom

It's worth repeating: Students are capable of more complex thought than they are typically asked to use. We have to be careful, though, not to take their initial responses as evidence of their abilities. Here's something every teacher knows: Initial student responses tend to be shallow, simple, and vague. It takes work and practice to make them deep, detailed, and profound. Even at a young age, students often form misunderstandings about how the world works. And these ideas are persistent. They need to be aware of this tendency and the problems associated with it: forgetting most things learned, lacking quality of thought, and inability to transfer learning to unfamiliar situations (to name a few).

> Students are capable of more complex thought than they are typically asked to use.

We need to be explicit from the start that the goal is **depth** of learning and **quality** of thought that organizes and transfers to new situations. It's not the

"Yep, got it, let's move on" that characterizes most coverage-centered classrooms. The older the students are, the more this habit takes time to unlearn.

The Foundation for Critical Thinking points out that human thought is naturally partial and biased. It takes practice to make it better. Students enter schools with preconceptions about ideas and topics that are usually simple and disconnected and are sometimes incorrect. These ideas tend to be *unconscious*. It's our job to help young people unearth them and improve them.

This idea is supported by rigorous research. The first principle from *How Students Learn: History, Mathematics, and Science in the Classroom,* published by the National Research Council (Donovan & Bransford, 2005), states,

> Students come to the classroom with preconceptions about how the world works. If their initial understanding is not engaged, they may fail to grasp the new concepts and information, or they may learn them for purposes of a test but revert to their preconceptions outside the classroom.

These findings have several implications for Concept-Based Instruction. The first is that students' understanding of conceptual relationships inevitably builds from their preconceptions about the concepts. Especially when our goal is to engage students through universal concepts like *change, system,* or *interdependence,* we must begin instruction by helping students become aware of their initial understanding of how these forces "work" in the world around them, so they can consciously improve their understanding by making it more clear, precise, accurate, and sophisticated.

A second implication is that we must make it clear to students and ourselves that Concept-Based Instruction is about *growth*. Students often think of learning as binary: Either I know something or I don't. This is because so much of their school experience is geared toward acquiring discrete pieces of factual knowledge—spelling and vocabulary tests, grammar drills, and mad-minute math quizzes all reinforce for kids what it feels like to "know" something as opposed to "not knowing." Developing conceptual understanding works differently. It is not as easy for students to tell when they've "got it." Giving lessons where students compare their understanding before and after, and showing them models of student work that increase in sophistication, will help them reorient their expectations of what learning feels like.

A third implication is that the learning environment must be one in which students feel comfortable exposing their own misunderstandings, changing their minds, and taking intellectual risks. The real work of conceptual learning involves admitting ignorance and seeking out one's own naivety, of making guesses and then rigorously testing them. An open, safe, supportive learning environment is essential.

This means that before we can successfully implement Concept-Based units and lessons, we must *take the time to orient student expectations of and approaches to learning.*

The following routines and strategies can be used to set the foundation for intellectual growth.

Strategy #3: Establish a positive community of learners.

Creating a community of trust is essential for risk taking and for harnessing the power of students learning from one another. It takes time and intentional effort to build trust and relationships within the classroom. Taking the time to do this will create an environment where students listen attentively and appreciate each other in a respectful manner.

Recent research demonstrates the importance of taking the time to establish a positive learning community. *The Harvard Men Study* followed 268 men from their entrance to college in the 1930s to present day. The study's director, George Vaillant, states that there are "70 years of evidence that our relationships with other people matter, and matter more than anything else in the world" (Vaillant, 2009, p. 2). Positive social relationships were the single most important determinant of success, health, and overall happiness of the men studied.

Shawn Anchor (2011), author of *The Happiness Advantage,* explains that a supportive group of people helps us to be more resilient and successful. In his own study he found that relationships and social support were greater predictors of happiness than GPA and income. Positive social interactions have been shown to significantly reduce depression, anxiety, and coronary heart disease! Here are some concrete ways you can establish a positive classroom community:

- Encourage **group problem solving**. Pose complicated questions, and allow students to work together on solving them.

- Teach **active listening**. Have students practice focusing on the speaker and the speaker's opinion and then asking interested questions to learn more. This might take lots of modeling and practice for younger students, but it's never too early to start learning how to be a good listener. You may want to give specific prompts, such as *look the person in the eye, nod your head*, et cetera. A specific strategy we like for older students is called triads: Students work on a particular question or topic in groups of three. Two students discuss or role-play, while the other student records observations to share with the rest of the class. Students take turns being the observer/recorder.

- **Share the research** with students. Let them reflect on the positive impacts of strong social connections.

- **Arrange desks** in groups, where students can face each other and work together. Placing a tall "inquiry table" at the center of the room, where it is surrounded by the desks or tables, is also good to entice curiosity and questions, as it is always visible as the centerpiece in the classroom. Depending on the unit of inquiry, the teacher can place a provocative objects or books on the table to support the unit that is being taught. Some teachers put sticky notes on the table for students to write questions on.

- Ask students to **describe their ideal class environment**. What makes learning fun? How might we encourage one another to work hard and keep going when we are learning big ideas? What can we do to make sure we are nice to one another? What could the teacher do? What should we avoid or not do? Create a poster of behaviors and attitudes to strive for, and a poster of behaviors and attitudes to avoid. Every few days, spend 10 minutes of class time reflecting on the extent to which the class is on track.

- Allow students to offer "shout-outs" to their peers for helping them understand an idea or achieve a goal. Use the simple framework, "I'd like to appreciate ___ for helping me understand ___."

Teachers have a tremendous amount of power to establish an emotionally safe space in every classroom. Below is a list of reflection questions to consider in pursuit of this important endeavor.

- Do I try to correct and redirect students privately rather than defaulting to public corrections? Try putting a hand on a shoulder, or whispering a redirection, rather than redirecting a child in front of the whole class.

- Do I work to ensure my classroom is an emotionally safe space, where teasing and laughing at others are not tolerated, and taking risks and learning from mistakes are the norms and expectations?

- Do I try to get to know each student on a personal level and use my relationship with each of them to motivate and inspire?

- Do I use examples and contexts that help students build positive identities for themselves?

- Which students get less patience from me, and how can I work toward giving them more patience and kindness?

Strategy #4: Intellectual journals.

Ask students to each keep a notebook or scrapbook that chronicles their intellectual journey and how their thinking has deepened and improved. You might explain how this will happen and what it will look like:

> We are going to collect evidence of our thinking in this class. Think of this as a scrapbook of what we are thinking as we explore different ideas. Each day we will record our ideas and thoughts as they develop. As the year goes by, you will be able to look back over your work to see your own intellectual growth.

Using intellectual journals is easy and can be adapted to meet the needs of any class structure. The basic principle is that students should be collecting their ideas about the concepts at various points in the unit. As their ideas evolve, their journal entries should become clearer, more precise, and more complex.

Early Elementary: Research suggests that even preschoolers can think about their thinking and be metacognitive about how to learn. We have experience with four- and five-year-olds who kept pictorial journals, and they have talked to each other and us about their scribbles in their journals. They motivated each other to work harder in their inquiry centers. You can also dedicate a wall space for this purpose as well as for group journals or scrapbooks. Take photos of students as they explore concepts. Ask them to draw how ideas are related. Capture things that they say, and review these with them regularly. Add materials and other evidence of things explored to their journals, and ask them to explain what these are and what they were thinking as they explored this evidence.

Middle to Upper Elementary: To use intellectual notebooks on a daily basis, start each class period with a question. As students begin class, ask them to write continuously in response to the question of the day for five minutes, and draw a line beneath their initial answer once time is up. Then ask them to repeat this procedure for the last five minutes of class to show how their thinking has changed as a result of their learning experiences.

Strategy #5: Partner coaching.

Most teachers have used a "think-pair-share" structure to encourage students to discuss their ideas with a partner. This variation moves beyond simple idea exchange, putting students in a position to help their partners grow as thinkers.

First, choose a conceptual question to explore, and then choose one of the coaching questions in Figure 2.4. Practice a few times with students before choosing another coaching question. Ask a student or fellow teacher or administrator to help model this process for the class. Explain the step as you model it. Then let the students try it out. Practice together as a class before releasing them on their own. For younger students, you might select two students to model it for the class a second time before releasing them to do it on their own. It might help to post the coaching question on the board and encourage older students to write down their partners' responses.

1. Pose a question and allow students time to think about their responses. For instance, you may put a conceptual question up on the board (How does the sun impact plants? or In what ways can we classify objects?) and give students five minutes to write freely or discuss with a partner.

2. Set up student pairs to coach each other toward improved thinking. Partner A should be allowed a few minutes to explain her answer, while Partner B listens. Then Partner B should coach Partner A by asking her questions to

push her thinking. After time is up, the partners should switch roles. After both rounds are up, all students should revise their original thinking by rewriting or restating their answers to the original prompt.

FIGURE 2.4 PARTNER COACHING PROTOCOL

Round 1:	Round 2:
Partner A explains her thinking.	Partner B explains his thinking.
Partner B asks questions to help develop Partner A's thoughts: • Could you explain what you mean a little more? • Could you give an example to show what you mean? • What are you most certain about? Least certain about? • What makes this difficult to explain or understand? • Why might someone disagree with what you're saying?	Partner A asks questions to help develop Partner B's thoughts: • Could you explain what you mean a little more? • Could you give an example to show what you mean? • What are you most certain about? Least certain about? • What makes this difficult to explain or understand? • Why might someone disagree with what you're saying?

Strategy #6: At first I thought . . . , but then . . . , so now I think. . . .

This simple template, adapted from *Making Thinking Visible: How to Promote Engagement, Understanding, and Independence for All Learners* (Ritchhart, Church, & Morrison, 2011), helps students identify their preconceptions and become aware of the way their understanding is changing as a result of their learning experiences. We like putting this sentence framework up on the board at the end of an activity or exploration and asking students to share out ways their thinking has changed. It is helpful to model the evolution of your own thinking as an example:

> Early Elementary: **At first I thought** that the taller the ramp the faster the car would go. **But then** Marco's ramp made me change my mind. Marco built a shorter ramp but it was more straight up than my ramp. (My teacher taught us a new word for this: *steep.*). **So now I think** the steeper the ramp, the faster the car will go.

> Middle to Upper Elementary: **At first I thought** that Wendy and her brothers should stay in Neverland. **But then** I saw how sad their mother was and how she missed them. It made me think of my own mom and how much I love her and she loves me. **So now I think** they were right to return home. Families belong together.

Doing this regularly encourages students to notice how they and their peers think and learn differently, and helps students gain metacognitive awareness of how their thoughts are changing in light of new information and experiences. Instead of asking students to share their thoughts verbally, you might ask students to write their responses on sticky notes and place them on the board at the end of a lesson. You can then read them and comment on the trends you see at the start of the next class.

Additional Strategies: Use these to help maintain a classroom culture where students support one another to become better thinkers.

- Make time in class for students to set personal goals for their learning and intellectual development. This is not the same as setting goals for grades or exam scores. Rather, these are goals about the type of thinking or understanding students want to achieve. For instance, one student may want to strengthen her ability to explain her ideas more fully. Another may be curious about women scientists. Ask students to write down or tell you so that you can write down their intellectual interests and goals. By reading them, you'll show that you care about students' individuality and that you consider them to be intellectual beings.

- Recognize students for their strong or improved thinking. This does not need to be elaborate or overly burdensome. Just pay attention to students' conversations and writing over the course of the week and jot down two or three specific examples of clear, accurate, precise, logical, or sophisticated thinking. Spend five minutes each Friday acknowledging these students and holding their work up as an example to others.

Teaching Students Explicitly About Conceptual Learning

As we noted in Chapter 1, this type of thinking comes naturally to very young children. It is done, however, on a subconscious level, and we need to take the time to help students get good at consciously abstracting big ideas from concrete examples and transferring them to completely new situations. We conclude from a number of important studies and researchers that it is extremely important to teach students explicitly about conceptual learning.

Clarke, Timperley, and Hattie (2003) say that an important feature of learning intentions and planning is that teachers share the learning intentions with students, so that they understand them and what success looks like. They caution that it is not as simple as students repeating the learning intention aloud at the start of the lesson. It is about taking the time to ensure they understand what success looks like and how the learning activities will prepare them for that success. Our experience has shown that this deeper understanding of what Concept-Based learning is has a tremendous impact on increasing students' motivation, deepening their learning, and making instruction more efficient.

Furthermore, researcher Robert Marzano (2007) emphasizes the importance of students having a clear understanding of the learning goals. He says, "Arguably, the most basic issue a teacher can consider is what he or she will do to establish and communicate learning goals" (p. 9). He goes on to say that because feedback is so powerful, learning goals are even more important. He says, "In fact, without clear goals it might be difficult to provide effective feedback" (p. 12). Hattie (2012) adds that "A key issue is that students often need to be explicitly taught the learning intentions and the success criteria" (p. 53). Chapter 5 will go into more detail about how to give effective feedback, but it relies on students knowing what deep, conceptual learning looks like.

The importance of student awareness of learning goals coupled with the important role of students monitoring their own learning leads us to believe that indeed, even very young students should understand explicitly what Concept-Based learning is and how it feels. The third principle from *How Students Learn* (Donovan & Bransford, 2005) states, "A 'metacognitive' approach to instruction can help students learn to take control of their own learning by defining learning goals and monitoring their progress in achieving them" (p. 2). We infer from these and other studies that students cannot adequately examine their progress without understanding key terms about Concept-Based learning.

Even very young children can understand that concepts help us to organize things. Students need time to think about the definition of a concept and how concepts are different from facts. They need time to practice evaluating and coming up with their own statements of conceptual relationship. After a few attempts, though, we've seen students shift not only their approach to learning, but their drive. When learning isn't just retelling what they heard from someone else, but instead is using their personal intellect to create their own understandings and unravel complex situations, it brings the joy back to learning. It is an investment of a couple class periods, but it will pay off! Consider the following classroom exercises as a way of helping students transition to conceptual learning.

Strategy #7: Building common Concept-Based language.

Although we have a natural tendency to abstract to the conceptual level, we do not come prewired with the ability to *consciously* distinguish facts from concepts, or with the understanding of how facts, concepts, and generalizations are related to each other. Therefore, it is worthwhile to spend a class period explaining the Structure of Knowledge and providing examples of the building blocks of conceptual learning.

Early Elementary: We should start with fostering their understanding that concepts help us to organize and categorize things. Children as young as two can categorize things they already know well, for example, toy trucks, cars, or airplanes, or pictures of these. We can write out two or three concept words and tell the students what the words are, or use objects to represent the broader concept. You could, for example, glue a tag with the concept word written on it, or a sample of an object that represents the concept, on a bag with at least two different concepts represented. Next, give students a bunch of different objects or pictures that correspond to the different concepts, and ask them to sort the mixed-up pictures according to the overarching concepts—or place them in the bag. You may also consider constructing a large board showing the Structure of Knowledge and adapt it to children's language. For example, instead of *facts,* call them *examples;* and instead of *concepts,* call them *ideas* or *categories.* The generalization could be called the *Big Idea.* This is an effective way of representing the Structure of Knowledge, and students quickly make connections to it. For example, in a social studies unit looking at the concept (or idea) of *celebrations,* students were able to give examples to support this concept. Eventually the concepts of *cultures* and *traditions* were introduced, and students were able to come up with a Big Idea (through the scaffolding of guiding questions) to support these concepts.

As they become better at sorting and categorizing items, experiment with some of the steps in the list that follows to see what they might be able to understand. You could gradually increase the level of abstraction in concepts, for example, from cars and trucks to vehicles and then transportation.

Middle to Upper Elementary: By the end of this exercise, students should be able to distinguish between facts and examples, topics, concepts, and generalizations about conceptual relationships. They should also come to see the difference between a strong and weak generalization, and to understand what we mean by "transfer."

1. Ask students, *What makes someone an expert? How are experts able to hold so much knowledge in their heads?* After students provide their initial thoughts, push them to think more deeply through a specific context:

   > Consider a veterinarian, a doctor for animals. Veterinary doctors must have a lot of knowledge about all the parts of many different animals. They must know how hundreds of medicines impact different animals differently and how these medicines interact with each other. They must learn several ways to help sick animals and be able to figure out what is wrong with each individual animal they see. How are they able to remember and use so much information?

   Students may come up with a variety of ideas: Veterinarians must read and study for many hours or years; veterinarians learn by applying what they know and learning from their mistakes; veterinarians learn by getting feedback from others.

2. Show students a diagram of the Structure of Knowledge. Tell students, *Many different factors go into developing expertise: time, experience, study. But the most important difference between an "expert" and a "beginner" is how the expert organizes the knowledge in her brain.* Ask students to examine the structure of knowledge diagram and hypothesize with a partner: *Consider this diagram that*

shows the way experts organize their knowledge. What do you notice? Why would experts think this way?

3. Teach them briefly about the components in the Structure of Knowledge using an example they already know and understand. The goal here is to establish a common understanding of what is meant by the terms *fact* versus *topic* versus *concept* versus *generalization*.

4. Give students a chance to practice telling the difference between facts and concepts. Ask them to sort discipline-specific terms into two piles: facts and concepts. Consider the list in Figure 2.5 for an English language arts classroom.

FIGURE 2.5   SAMPLE CONCEPTS AND FACTS FROM ENGLISH LANGUAGE ARTS

Facts/examples:	Concepts:
Captain Hook	Villain
Peter Pan	Hero
Tinker Bell	Character
Sleeping Beauty	Plot
Prince Charming	Destiny

5. Show students statements of conceptual relationships (generalizations or principles), and ask, "What are they? How do they help us organize information? How do they help us figure out new situations?"

6. To improve statements of conceptual relationships, show students statements with a few with weak verbs and proper nouns, and ask students to fix the statements. Show them that asking "how" or "why" often helps us to make statements stronger. Asking "so what" increases the statements' significance. For instance, consider the increasing complexity in the generalizations below:

- Villains and heroes are two important concepts in stories.

- Heroes typically defeat villains in stories.

- The plot of many stories follows a similar development where the hero fulfills his destiny by finally defeating an evil villain, telling the lesson that good usually wins over evil.

Model briefly for students how a strong generalization can be built going "up" the Structure of Knowledge.

7. To facilitate transfer, show students new situations. Ask them which conceptual relationship best unlocks the new situation and discuss why or how.

8. To help students come up with their own statements, tell them, "We can abstract our own statements by asking ourselves, 'What is the relationship between two or more of the concepts?' and use the facts to help us answer. Give them the sentence starter, *I understand that. . . .*

9. As a final reflection, ask the students to again articulate the difference between a concept and a fact. How is learning about a concept different from learning about a fact? What is the definition of and importance of conceptual relationships? How do we improve statements of conceptual relationships? What are some ways to discover conceptual relationships? How do they help us to unlock unfamiliar situations?

Obviously, these learning exercises are best suited for early in the school year, as they are focused on introducing the idea of conceptual learning for the first time. But the same principles can be applied at any point in the year, even in the middle of a unit! The truth is that students can do a better job at conceptualizing ideas for which they already have a deep fact base. Figure 2.6 is an example of the steps in a third-grade class. The students had already been learning details about their city, Washington, DC.

FIGURE 2.6   INTRODUCING CONCEPT-BASED LEARNING—SAMPLE THIRD-GRADE SOCIAL STUDIES LESSON

1. **Students discuss in pairs: What makes someone an expert?** How do they remember so much? Teacher records responses on the board. Teacher says, *I'm going to let you in on a little secret about experts. They organize information in their heads through something called the Structure of Knowledge. This helps them to remember things more easily and helps them to unlock new situations on their own. You have already begun learning in this way; we are just going to be direct from now on about this type of thinking and learning.*

2. **Teacher shows the Structure of Knowledge** (or Structure of Process if you teach language, arts, or music), using their current unit as an example. Starting from the topic level and the facts (Anacostia River, White House, Washington Monument), the teacher briefly explains each component, ending with the concepts (built features, natural features, ways of life) and the statement of conceptual relationship: The built and natural features of a place shape the way people live.

3. **Students sort concepts and facts into piles:** Then they come up with a working definition of each category—they will probably say things like concepts are more "general" and facts are more "specific." This is a great opportunity to teach them the word *abstract* as one of the key definitions of concepts. In this case each small group gets two piles of images or words of examples in the concepts. The concepts are in italics just for you to see but would be the same size so students have to figure out which one is different for each pile. They already have experience with these facts and concepts, so this should be pretty easy to do. The point is to see the difference between concepts and facts. *Built features*: Capitol Building, White House, Washington Monument, Memorial Bridge, 14th Street Bridge; *natural features*: Anacostia River, Potomac River, Rock Creek Park

4. **Statements of conceptual relationship:** Each small group gets the following two statements:
   - People tend to settle and make towns and cities on rivers because they are important for transportation using boats and ships.

- People sometimes construct buildings and monuments to communicate messages such as respect or power.

They discuss these questions about the statements: What are they? How do they help us organize information? How would they help us figure out new situations without the teacher there to help us?

5. **Improving statements of conceptual relationship:** Teacher starts with the basics—no proper nouns, no weak verbs (*is, are, have, impact, affect, influence*). Teacher explains the rationale behind these guidelines: Proper nouns are facts—they don't transfer; weak verbs don't tell us enough about the relationship between two or more concepts. Students evaluate these statements and improve them:

- The buildings in Washington, DC, communicate power.
- Rivers impact traffic in major cities.

6. **Synergistic thinking:** Students receive the following statements and facts, mixed up, and discuss them in groups. Which facts best support each generalization? Do any of the facts challenge or complicate the generalizations? Teacher explains the power of synergistic thinking.

- Access to natural features enhances the beauty of a place. (Anacostia River, Rock Creek Park)
- Beautifully constructed manmade features can bring tourists to a place. (White House, Washington Monument, World War II Memorial)

7. **Transfer:** Teacher shows students maps and pictures from a new city that they have not seen, such as Paris or London. They are to choose which of the statements in Item 6 above best helps them to unlock the new situation and why.

8. **Writing our own statements:** Teacher tells students that we abstract our own statements by asking ourselves, "What is the relationship between two or more of the concepts?" and use the facts to help us answer it. They try it out with "What is the relationship between natural and manmade features and the way people live?" They have to answer it in their own words. Teacher gives them the sentence starter, *I understand that _____.*

9. **Reflection:** Spend as much time on this as possible through discussion.

- What is the difference between a concept and a fact?
- How is learning about a concept different from learning about a fact?
- What is the definition of and importance of conceptual relationships?
- How do we improve statements of conceptual relationships?
- What are some ways to discover conceptual relationships?
- How do they help us to unlock unfamiliar situations?

Strategy #8: Contrasting traditional learning with Concept-Based learning.

Ask students to consider the two panels of images in Figure 2.7. Both panels present metaphors for learning. In the first panel, traditional learning is likened to collecting pebbles on the beach, while in the second, Concept-Based learning is likened to chiseling a sculpture from a rough piece of marble. This step might be too abstract for very young students, but you can always try it out and see if they can get it.

FIGURE 2.7   TRADITIONAL LEARNING VERSUS CONCEPT-BASED LEARNING

SOURCE: Jimmy Conde, graphic artist.

In the traditional model of learning, students play a rather passive role, waiting for the teacher to point out the facts and ideas they should "collect" in their jars. The goal of this type of learning is for students to hold all the facts in their heads until the end of the year (or until the day of the test), at which point they dump out the ideas they have learned to prove they have retained them. This type of learning does not invite students to shape the ideas or construct their own meaning; rather, students' minds are seen as empty jars waiting to be filled with the ideas of others.

Contrast this with the Concept-Based learning process, where students begin not with empty vessels, but rather with their own preexisting ideas symbolized by the mound of rough stone waiting to be sculpted. In conceptual learning, we begin with what we already know and work to refine our ideas through disciplined study. As we learn, our ideas become more sophisticated, clear, precise, complex, and accurate, just as the sculpture takes on more nuanced form with each chisel mark. In the end, the product of our learning is a profound, well-thought-out idea of our own construction (not a jar full of details the teacher has asked us to memorize).

We like this exercise because it strengthens students' ability to think symbolically and metaphorically and provides an easy touchstone for later reference: *Remember we're sculpting masterpieces, not collecting pebbles.* Here are the basic steps:

1. Assign students to work with a partner. One student should be Partner A and one should be Partner B.

2. Ask student pairs to first describe each panel, and then discuss the ways in which each panel might serve as a metaphor for learning. You might say something like this:

> Today we are going to think about the difference between traditional learning and conceptual learning. To begin with, let's consider these two panels of images. Each one offers a metaphor for what it is like to learn at school. Let's see if you can figure out how these panels relate to learning. If you are Partner A, raise your hand. Partner A, you are going to focus on the top panel. I would like you to study your panel silently for one minute. Notice as many details as you can; after one minute you will explain the top panel to your partner. Partner B, raise your hand. Partner B, while your partner studies the top panel, you will focus on the bottom panel. Notice as many details as you can; after one minute you will explain the bottom panel to your partner.

This is essentially a think-pair-share strategy, which we like because it ensures that every student has a specific role in the discussion (as either Partner A or Partner B) and, therefore, must take responsibility for the thinking in the lesson. As students discuss, circulate to monitor their discussions and offer quick prompts to groups that finish prematurely, signaling to them that the goal is not to "finish" the conversation but rather to **sustain their thinking in order to deepen it**.

3. Call on students to describe each panel in detail. After students share out their initial thoughts, probe for deeper thinking:
   - The first panel compares the learning process to collecting pebbles in a jar, while the second compares the learning process to sculpting a masterpiece from a mound of rock. Have you ever experienced learning that relates to either of these metaphors? Let's share out some examples.

- What role does the student play in the learning process in each panel? The teacher? What are the pros and cons to each model?
- In the first panel, the student begins with an empty jar. In the second panel, the student begins with a rough mound of rock. Why is this an important difference?
- What product does the student end up with in the first panel? The second? Which type of learning seems more valuable?

4. Ask students to compare traditional learning with conceptual learning in writing. For the very young, the teacher can do this as a whole class and use the board to write their ideas. Have them open to a new page in their notebooks and divide it in half. On the top half, they should write a paragraph that describes traditional learning. On the bottom half, they should write a paragraph that shows how Concept-Based learning is different. We like to use the model from the Foundation for Critical Thinking (Paul & Elder, 2013) for writing explanatory paragraphs: State, Elaborate, Exemplify, Illustrate (SEEI for short). The sentence stems in Figure 2.8 offer a strong model for students to use as they think through a concept or idea:

FIGURE 2.8   SEEI TEMPLATE

(State the idea clearly) Traditional learning is all about . . . .

(Elaborate on the idea) In other words, the goal of traditional learning is. . . . During the learning process, students mainly . . . while teachers mainly . . . . In the end, the product of student learning is . . . .

(Exemplify) For example, ...

(Illustrate with a metaphor or image) It's like . . . .

(State the difference clearly) On the other hand, conceptual learning is all about . . . .

(Elaborate on the idea) In other words, the goal of conceptual learning is not . . . but rather. . . . During the conceptual learning process, students . . . while teachers . . . . In the end, the product of conceptual learning is . . . .

(Exemplify) For example, ...

(Illustrate with a metaphor or image) It's like . . . .

SOURCE: Paul, R., & Elder, L. (2013). *The thinker's guide to how to write a paragraph: The art of substantive writing.* Tomales, CA: Foundation for Critical Thinking.

Unleashing the Power of Iterative Learning

Most traditional learning is linear. Think about a set of standards or a textbook. The underlying assumption seems to be that students will move on from topic to topic, fact to fact, in a straightforward sequence. Students accumulate knowledge by moving from one standard or chapter to the next, checking each one off as they go.

Although the topics and facts may be carefully ordered to create a logical, progressive path through the course, rarely is emphasis placed on the connections among topics, facts, and ideas.

We need to be explicit about how Concept-Based learning might be different from what students are used to doing, especially for older students who are used to a more topic-based, coverage-centered classroom. Even if young kids don't have too many preconceptions about how learning works, most teachers went through at least 16+ years of schooling that was probably very coverage based. It is important to do our own reflecting on the ways in which our schooling impacts what we think is good teaching.

Parker Palmer (1998) states, in *The Courage to Teach,*

> If we teachers are to help form our students in the image of truth, we must attend to our own re-formation. Having had our vision shaped by one-eyed education, and working under conditions that discourage us from opening the other eye, we are in special need of exercises that can help us see and be whole.

It might be great to do the following exercises first with a group of teachers, or on your own for your own self-reflection, before conducting them with students.

Here's how a linear classroom works: Each day the teacher posts an objective or goal to be achieved during the lesson. Lesson activities are designed to allow students to meet the daily goal, and students are responsible for mastering a "chunk" of content or a specific skill each day. After two or three weeks, students take a test that covers each of the daily goals from the unit. For instance, a week in a third-grade health class might consist of the activities shown in Figure 2.9.

FIGURE 2.9   SAMPLE HEALTH UNIT (TRADITIONAL)

Unit: Healthy Eating
- Day 1: Students will explain the difference between foods with nutrients and foods without nutrients.
- Day 2: Students will classify foods as predominantly carbohydrates, proteins, or fats.
- Day 3: Students will analyze the impacts of carbohydrates, proteins, and fats on the human body.
- Day 4: Students will describe the impacts of unhealthy eating and the steps to form better habits.
- Day 5: Students will create plans for making healthy eating choices.

Notice that while the daily lessons proceed in a logical order, the goal of each lesson is still discrete and self-contained. The most intuitive students may grasp a larger structure or trajectory for their learning, but for most students the content appears episodic, segmented, and partial. There is rarely time to go back to the content of previous lessons in order to revise or challenge one's thinking. Every lesson is a move forward with new content, new goals.

Conceptual learning is not linear; it's iterative. By this we mean that learning happens through repetitions of the inquiry process, giving students multiple chances to develop ideas and deepen their understanding relative to a single learning goal. Consider the unit outlined in Figure 2.10.

FIGURE 2.10   SAMPLE HEALTH UNIT (CONCEPT-BASED)

> Unit: Choices and Decision Making in the Context of Healthy Eating
> Generalization: Healthy food choices can lead to a better life.
>
> **Question: How do choices about food impact our lives?**
> Inquiry cycles:
> * Context #1: Physical shape and weight
> * Context #2: Energy
> * Context #3: Sleep and mood
> * Context #4: Immune system

Much of the content included in the Concept-Based unit is the same as that included in the traditional, linear unit. Both units will expose students to specific nutrients found in foods and their impacts on the body. The difference is that the *goal* of learning each day in the Concept-Based unit is to deepen student understanding of the relationships among concepts. In this case, students are coming to understand the larger concept of choices—the process by which a person controls his or her own life—in relation to food and health. Choice is a concept that students will come back to again and again in health class as they study everything from peer pressure to addiction, giving them many chances to make meaning of this concept for themselves. Students will investigate several contexts, but this learning is far from episodic or disconnected. The concepts and iterative cycle of inquiry lend coherence and purpose to the learning.

Moreover, each context increases in complexity over the previous context. In the case of this health unit, the second context regarding energy introduces greater complexity when students learn about the ways in which the body breaks down food and what it does with it. In the third context, another element of complexity is added when students study the impact of nutrients on the body's need for sleep and the regulation of our mood. The final context adds complexity when students investigate the basics of our immune system and how food powers it or impairs it.

Strategy #9: Linear versus iterative learning processes.

It is important to help students understand that iterative learning is organized differently than linear learning. Many students expect and even enjoy "checklist" learning, because it feels productive and concrete. They may feel frustrated by iterative learning at first, because the learning goal can never be "checked off" the list. This activity helps students understand and come to appreciate the iterative learning process.

FIGURE 2.11   ITERATIVE VERSUS LINEAR LEARNING PROCESSES

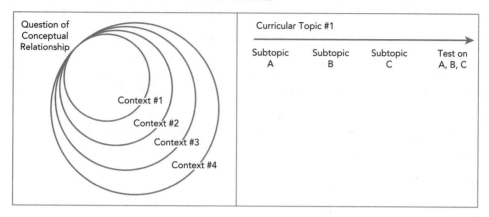

1. Display the two images in Figure 2.11 for the class, and ask students to describe the differences they see. Together, list words that seem to describe each image. Here are a few key differences and observations to get you started:

Iterative learning	Linear learning
Interlocking circles	Straight line
Moving in a repeated cycle	Moving step-by-step
Always returning to a conceptual question	Always moving forward
Distinct contexts united by concepts	Broken down into subtopics
Each context is larger/more complicated than the previous one	A leads to B, B leads to C

2. Present students with the following scenarios. Ask them which scenario relates more closely to the iterative process.

> Scenario A: Students are learning how to bake cakes. The teacher gives students the recipe for vanilla cake, students measure out and combine the ingredients, and then students bake the cake. The teacher tastes each cake to determine if students got it right.

> Scenario B: Students are learning how to bake cakes. First, students bake a vanilla cake using flour, sugar, eggs, baking powder, milk, and vanilla. They evaluate the taste and texture of the

cake, noting its characteristics. Then students bake a second cake, this time adding butter, and again evaluate the taste and texture of their final product. Later, students bake a third cake using oil instead of butter, noting how this changes the cake. They continue to experiment with changes to the recipe until they have gotten the taste and texture just right.

3. Discuss the pros and cons of each type of learning. For instance, students may note that iterative learning promotes discovery through experimentation and focuses on refining an idea or process. This gives students more agency in the learning process. They might worry, though, that learning this way will feel repetitive. They will likely note that linear learning is more straightforward, but also less likely to produce learning that is deep or lasting.

Strategy #10: Simple versus sophisticated, static versus dynamic ideas.

Teaching through the iterative process described in this chapter only works if students know what it looks like to increase the sophistication of their thinking about the concepts. Many teachers get frustrated when student thinking remains stagnant, and instruction seems only to reinforce shallow, superficial views of the concepts. *Why do we keep having the same discussion every single day, no matter the context we're studying?* The answer is simple: This is what kids expect from their learning experiences. School very often rewards kids for matching, not understanding, ideas.

Think about a group of first-grade students studying the concepts of number and quantity using counting chips and other objects. They can define the concepts, recall examples, and recognize them. But if we want them to actually deepen their understanding, we need to look at increasingly complex situations where the concepts are present—and kids need to be explicitly clued in to this purpose. Here is one way to help students understand the purpose of studying the concepts in various contexts through an iterative process. We purposefully chose a topic that is appropriate for younger grades, to show that this exercise can be done with young children—with careful scaffolding and modifications.

Early Elementary: Use the images from Figure 2.11 to correspond to the ideas of the two different types of learning. (The circles show sophisticated and dynamic learning, and the straight line shows simple and static learning.) Select the simpler terms from Figure 2.12—for example, use the terms *remaining the same* and *constant change or progress* instead of using *static* and *dynamic,* respectively. Lead a whole-class discussion to compare and contrast the ideas. Act out the scenario in Figure 2.13 instead of having students read it, and discuss as a class after each inquiry cycle. For Step 3, you can make up stories that show how a new learning experience or new information confirms, contradicts, or complicates understanding.

Middle to Upper Elementary:

1. Develop common definitions of the terms *simple, sophisticated, static,* and
    dynamic. Ask students to fold a piece of paper in half, and then in half again,
    to create four even boxes. Have them write the definition of one term in
    each box. Then, working with a partner, each student should list as many
    synonyms for each term as possible. The result might look something like
    this:

FIGURE 2.12   DIFFERENCES BETWEEN SIMPLE AND SOPHISTICATED LEARNING

Simple: basic	Sophisticated: complex
• Uncomplicated • Naïve • Unaware • Easy, presenting no difficulty • Straightforward • Obvious • Plain	• Nuanced • Informed, knowledgeable • Consisting of many parts • Difficult • Fully thought out • Multifaceted
Static: remaining the same	Dynamic: characterized by constant change or progress
• Fixed • Unchanging • Immobile or not moving • Stuck • Stable	• Always improving • Growing • Never settling • Active

2. Present the two student portraits in Figure 2.13, and ask students which
    portrayed student seems to be developing a sophisticated, dynamic
    understanding.

3. When moving through each cycle of inquiry, students should be looking for
    ways the information can do each of the following:
    *   *Confirm* their understanding
    *   *Contradict* their understanding
    *   *Qualify* their understanding
    *   *Complicate* their understanding

Discuss what each of these terms means and might look like. Ask students, *When did
Student B find information to confirm her understanding? Contradict it? Qualify or complicate it? What was the result? How did this make her ideas more sophisticated and dynamic?*

Introduce students to these phrases dealing with exceptions, nuances, and conditions. Ask students to brainstorm other phrases that might help them avoid overly
simplistic thinking.

FIGURE 2.13   SIMPLE/STATIC IDEAS VERSUS SOPHISTICATED/DYNAMIC IDEAS

What is the relationship between number and quantity?

Student A initial response:

Numbers show quantities.

Student B initial response:

Numbers show quantities.

Inquiry Cycle #1: Objects

Students use counting chips, cubes, balls, and their fingers to explore number and quantity. They notice that there is a difference between more and less as well as bigger and smaller when comparing groups of objects.

Student A:

Yep! I was right! Numbers show quantities. When I had four counting chips they show the number 4. When I put up four fingers, they show the number 4.

Student B:

Hmm. I see. Numbers are used to represent different amounts or quantities in the real world. Seven counting chips shows more than three counting chips. More means a bigger quantity, and that can be shown with numbers instead of using the actual objects.

Inquiry Cycle #2: Dots

Students use cards and dice with dots to continue to explore number and quantity. They notice that the dots on an object (cards or dice) make it a little harder to compare numbers, because they can't remove the dots and line them up.

Student A:

Yep! I was right! Numbers show quantities. The dots show a quantity that has a number to show that quantity. A dice with a quantity of five dots shows the number 5.

Student B:

I'm noticing that whenever a quantity is represented on a card or die, we can memorize the corresponding number in order to recognize it faster. Now when someone rolls a die, I can quickly tell the number it represents without having to count the dots one by one.

Inquiry Cycle #3: Lines

Students learn about the number line using games such as Chutes and Ladders and a Human Game Map to further explore the relationship between number and quantity. They notice that numbers can represent both a specific spot on the line and a number of *moves* along the line.

Student A:

Yep! I was right! Numbers show a quantity. Four spaces along the number line show the number 4.

Student B:

Number lines are interesting and a little more complicated. When we add more or less of a quantity, it's like moving forward or backward along a number line.

SOURCE: Math content adapted from Donovan & Bransford (2005).

use ?s on
p 29

TOOLS FOR TEACHING CONCEPTUAL UNDERSTANDING, ELEMENTARY

- If . . . then. . . .
- Only when . . . .
- But . . . .
- Unless . . . .
- If . . . had . . . , then the result would change to . . . .
- An exception to this is . . . .

Conclusion

At the start of this chapter, we outlined four simple yet powerful principles for setting the foundation for a Concept-Based classroom:

1. We can honor developmental stages of childhood with intellectual rigor.
2. Conceptual learning happens best in a student-centered, thinking-centered classroom.
3. It is important to teach students explicitly about how to learn conceptually.
4. Conceptual learning is iterative; students need chances to refine and increase the sophistication of their thinking.

For many teachers, the biggest "Aha!" moment comes when they realize that Concept-Based classrooms operate differently than traditional coverage-based classrooms, and that students need to be made aware of these differences. We have found that few teachers deliberately clue students in to the purpose of their learning or explain the intentionality behind the instructional activities planned. Investing the time to build a thinking classroom, where students know how to learn conceptually and come to expect the iterative learning process, will pay dividends later.

Chapter Review

- How can I create a student-centered, thinking-centered classroom? What problems might I encounter along the way?
- What strategies can I use to orient student expectations of learning and teach students how to learn conceptually?
- What makes iterative learning so powerful? How can I make sure that students' understanding is grown deeper and more complex through each inquiry cycle?

....

What Are the Building Blocks of Concept-Based Instruction?

The previous chapter outlines our recommendations for establishing the foundation necessary for a Concept-Based classroom. For instruction to work, teachers must first create a thinking-centered classroom where students expect iterative learning and understand that the goal is to develop sophisticated and transferable understandings.

Next, we turn our attention to the instructional principles that guide conceptual teachers in designing learning experiences for their students:

1. We need to expose students' **preinstructional understanding** of the concepts and conceptual relationship.
2. A deep understanding of **each concept by itself** is necessary for a sophisticated understanding of the relationship among several concepts.
3. Students must **uncover** the conceptual relationship for themselves.
4. **Transfer** is both a means to and an end of conceptual learning.

Starting With Students' Preinstructional Understandings

In their groundbreaking report for teachers, *How Students Learn: History, Mathematics, and Science in the Classroom*, Donovan and Bransford (2005) remind us of a basic truth about learning:

> Students come to the classroom with preconceptions about how the world works. If their initial understanding is not engaged, they may

fail to grasp the new concepts and information, or they may learn them for purposes of a test but revert to their preconceptions outside the classroom. (p. 1)

This is especially important for conceptual teachers. Our ultimate goal is to develop deep and lasting understanding in our students so that they can use their learning to tackle big, messy real-world challenges ranging from climate change to domestic violence. Research tells us that in order to reach this goal, we must first expose, and then deal directly with, the preinstructional understandings students bring with them each day.

Another reason that starting with students' preinstructional understandings is so important is that it allows us to track growth in students' understanding of the concepts and conceptual relationships at the heart of a unit of study. If we fail to make students' prior understanding visible early on, it is entirely possible that they coast through a lesson or entire unit without actually learning anything new. Without a record of students' initial thinking about the concepts, neither teacher nor student really knows the impact of a learning experience. Did students gain a deeper, clearer, more precise, or more sophisticated understanding of the concepts? Without a baseline, we have no way to tell.

Gauging students' preinstructional understanding does not need to be fancy or take up much instructional time. Consider the usefulness of the strategies below—many of them are not new, but we have adapted them specifically for uncovering preinstructional understanding of conceptual thinking.

Strategy #1: Individual journaling.

- Post a simple conceptual question, or series of questions, on the board for students to consider.
- Ask them to respond to the question(s) in their journals.

It is important that all students have time to think and write something substantive about the concepts before time is up, so be sure to monitor student responses and encourage reluctant writers. For an exercise like this, be intentional in the composition of your questions. It may be helpful to consider a variety of question types, such as those captured in Figure 3.1. Think about which questions would best spark student thought and elicit the understandings you are looking for.

After students have a chance to write, it is often helpful for students to make their understandings visible to each other:

- Ask students to share their responses with a partner, looking for similarities and differences in their ideas.

- Call on several students at random and ask them to share their ideas with the whole class. After each student shares, ask others to agree or disagree or to provide related examples.

- For debatable questions, take a quick poll to see the spread of opinions across the class.

FIGURE 3.1   SAMPLE CONCEPTUAL QUESTIONS

Defining Well-Known Concepts	Defining Lesser-Known Concepts	Understanding Relationships	Debating Relationships
What is your definition of *responsibility?* Give an example. Does *duty* mean the same as *responsibility?* Why or why not? How would you define it?	Have you ever heard the term *equality* before? What do you think this concept means? Is it ever fair to treat people differently, or is it most fair to treat everyone the same? Explain your thinking.	How are rules and responsibility related? What is the relationship between rules and equality? How are these concepts different? How are they similar?	Which is more important for a community: rules or responsibility? Do rules naturally produce responsibility? In order to achieve equality, is it necessary to have rules?

Strategy #2: Four corners.

Another strategy for making student understanding visible to the entire class is a four corners activity. We love this one because it combines physical movement with the requirement that every student must respond to the question at hand.

The procedure is simple:

1. Post a conceptual question in multiple-choice format for students to consider. We like to start with the stem, "Which of the following best matches your understanding of _____?" This works for gauging understanding of individual concepts as well as conceptual relationships. Here is an example:

    Which of the following best matches your understanding of *metaphor?*

    a. A comparison between two things

    b. A figure of speech that matches one thing to another

    c. Making two things equal to each other

    d. A thing regarded as representative or symbolic of something else

2. Give students a few minutes of silent thinking time. Set a timer, if only for yourself, and do not allow students to share their answers prematurely. It's important that all students have a chance to consider the question for themselves. Also, students who experience an initial "gut reaction" to the question will have time to reconsider as they think things through. We also find it useful to have students write down an answer during the silent thinking time, especially if we suspect that students might change their answers once they see where their peers are moving.

3. Assign each answer to a corner of the classroom. You may even want to post one answer in each corner using chart paper. Ask students to vote with their feet by moving to the corner of the answer they chose.

4. Have each group discuss the reasoning behind their choice, and ask representatives of each group to share out to the whole class. Or, to boost a low-energy class, have each corner group try to recruit members of the other groups by arguing the merits of their answer choice.

Strategy #3: Take a stand; then divide and slide.

To tap further into students' affinity for debate, consider posing a debatable question (one with two clear, opposing answers) or posting a statement with which students can agree or disagree.

After some thinking time, ask students to "take a stand" on the question and then "divide and slide" before debating their position. Here are the steps:

1. Give students a few minutes of silent thinking time to consider your debatable question or agree/disagree statement. For instance, the teacher may ask students,

   *Which is more important for a community: **rules** or **responsibility**?*

   or the teacher may offer the choice either to agree or disagree with the statement,

   Oral presentations are more persuasive than written texts.

2. Ask students to take a stand on the question by physically lining up along a spectrum of answer choices. In the case of the question above, one end of the spectrum would be the answer choice "rules" and the other end would be "responsibility." In the case of the statement, one end of the spectrum would be the answer choice "agree" and the other end "disagree." The desired result is one single-file line, so it may help to ask students to line up against a wall or along a line of tape adhered to the floor. It also helps to post a visual on the board (like the one in Figure 3.2).

Once students have formed a single-file line along the "take a stand" spectrum, divide the line exactly in half and ask all students on one side to take a giant step away from the line. Students should still be in the same single-file order, but now they form two separate lines, as shown in Figure 3.3.

FIGURE 3.2

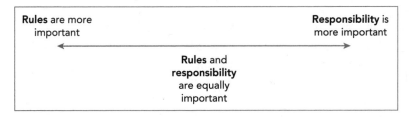

FIGURE 3.3

Next, have one half of the line "slide" toward the other half so now they are standing in two parallel lines. Each student should have a partner across from them in the opposite line whose views on the question are different from their own. This formation is shown in Figure 3.4.

FIGURE 3.4

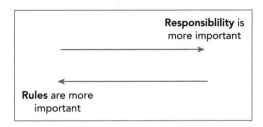

Finally, ask students to share their position on the question and reasoning behind it with the partner across from them in the opposite line. Or, to add some excitement, ask them to engage in a minidebate with their partner by giving each side one or two minutes to make the case for their position. Take the time to notice where students line up and to listen in on their discussions or debates to gauge the range of understandings in the class.

1. We always like to ask students to record their responses to the conceptual question in writing before moving on. The "take a stand and divide and slide" activity makes their thoughts visible for a short period of time, but it is important to have a written snapshot of their thinking to look back to later in the unit of study. Provide a few minutes of silent journaling time to wrap up the activity.

Strategy #4: Gallery walk with chalk talk.

Another way to get students up and moving while capturing their initial understanding of the concepts is to conduct a gallery walk activity that invites students to record their thinking by writing responses to others' thinking on poster paper around the room. This strategy is often called "chalk talk" even though you will probably be using markers.

1. Set up several pieces of poster paper around the room, each with a separate conceptual question on it. Consider including a variety of questions, such as those in Figure 3.1, to elicit different types of thinking from students at each station. Students will be rotating around the room, writing out their answers on each poster, so make sure there is plenty of blank space for student responses.

2. Assign each student a poster as a starting place, with no more than three students at any given poster. For a large class, we like to make duplicate posters so that students can spread out and have space to write even if the questions on many of the posters are the same. More than three per poster is just too crowded. At their first poster, students should spend some time thinking about the question and then write a thoughtful answer before signing their name.

3. At each subsequent poster, students should begin by reading what their peers have written and then respond. Encourage students to respond directly to one another, either by agreeing and adding on, disagreeing with a reason, or asking a question. The goal is to engage in a written conversation and explore ideas. You may want to post the following sentence starters to help keep them on track:
    *   I agree with Maria and would like to add that . . . .
    *   I disagree, Sean, because . . . .
    *   Jasmine's comment makes me wonder . . . .

4. Once students have made a full lap of the room, they should return to their original poster to read the responses that have accumulated during the activity. Ask one spokesperson per poster to share the most common, unique, or interesting ideas they find there.

One of the reasons we like the gallery walk with chalk talk is that it's the perfect bookend activity. At the end of the unit, put the posters back up and ask students to walk back through to find their original responses. Have them reply to themselves using sticky notes or a different color marker. Afterward, they can journal about how their thinking has changed over the course of their learning.

This brings us to an important point: Although we've listed these strategies as ways to engage students' prior understanding of concepts, the same activities can be used throughout a Concept-Based unit to gauge student progress. They are fun and interactive. Plus, once students have done them a few times, they can be executed quite efficiently, taking up no more than 15 minutes of instructional time.

Introducing New Concepts

The first five strategies in this chapter assume that the concepts you're dealing with are somewhat familiar to students. For instance, we've used the concepts of rules and responsibility as examples of common concepts that students are likely to know from previous contexts.

But in order to achieve depth of understanding and disciplinary competence, students also need to learn new concepts with which they have had no prior encounters. For instance, math students must come to understand the concept of **fractions**, English students will need to learn the concept of **setting**, and social studies students should develop awareness of the concept of **region.** Although it may be helpful to expose students' prior understandings of *related* concepts—the concept of **division** before studying fractions, or the concepts of **cities** and **states** before studying region—most students will have little pre-instructional understanding of the discipline-specific concepts listed here.

When introducing a new concept, the biggest pitfall is treating it like a fact. Many teachers instinctively want to teach concepts like vocabulary words, offering textbook definitions and then quizzing kids on those definitions later. The problem here is that students struggle to distinguish meaningfully between concepts and facts on their own. Left to their own devices, they'll dutifully go home and memorize definitions without really understanding much at all. Then they—and their teachers—will be disappointed when they can't apply or analyze or evaluate based on the concepts.

Helping students *understand* a concept means more than knowing a definition. Consider using the see-think-wonder, concept attainment and SEEI (state, elaborate, exemplify, illustrate) strategies that follow to encourage more than memorization.

Strategy #5: See-think-wonder.

Here is another great strategy directly from *Making Thinking Visible: How to Promote Engagement, Understanding, and Independence for All Learners* (Ritchhart, Church, & Morrison, 2011). It is incredibly simple and incredibly engaging. How often do we find both of those things in one strategy?! We find it to be a great way to introduce a new concept.

Looking at an image or object,

- What do you **see**?
- What do you **think** is going on?
- What does it make you **wonder**?

This strategy helps to create interest and student-generated questions. It is imperative to clarify what is really going on in the image or object to clear up any misconceptions that may have surfaced during the discussion. We like to follow it with the next strategy, which goes into more depth about the critical attributes of a concept.

Strategy #6: Concept attainment.

Concept attainment lessons are super easy to plan, and kids love them because it feels like they're putting together the clues in a mystery. The steps below mimic the brain's natural concept-formation process by drawing out patterns from examples and nonexamples:

1. **Examples:** The goal of a concept attainment lesson is for students to develop their own "definition" of a concept by investigating many examples. This works particularly well for discipline-specific concepts to which students won't have had a lot of previous exposure, or for which their prior understanding is likely naive or incomplete. For instance,

   - Young science students are asked what it means for something to be living. After writing down their initial guess, the teacher shows several slides of living things. The first might be a human, then several animals. Kids may guess that living things run, eat, and breathe. Then the teacher may show pictures of trees, flowers, and mosses, and kids may need to revise their answer in light of the new examples, since these plants cannot run. Perhaps they notice that all of these things grow, so they add that to the list. The class continues this way with progressively more nuanced examples. Students are challenged to alter their definitions when the teacher shows pictures of pinecones and roadkill (since, in science, "living" refers to anything that is or has been alive).

   - **History** students are studying leadership. They start by reading four short descriptions of American leaders—George Washington, Abraham Lincoln, Frederick Douglass, and Eleanor Roosevelt. Knowing that these are all examples of leaders, they look for common traits. They may notice that the first two were presidents but, upon reading about Douglass, will reject this as a characteristic of leadership because Douglass and Roosevelt were not elected leaders. But they might be savvy enough to notice that all of these people had influence on the nation.

   What we *love* about this step is that usually history students would be reading about George Washington and Eleanor Roosevelt with the intention of highlighting and memorizing the dates and details about their lives. But they are so much more engaged when we explain to them that their goal is *not* to find and memorize these terms, which are *facts*, but rather to use these facts to investigate the larger *concept*.

2. **Distinguishing examples from nonexamples:** After students have working definitions (usually lists of criteria) for the target concept, they practice applying these definitions to more examples and nonexamples.

   - The science teacher gives groups of students a bunch of photographs of living and nonliving things. Using their definitions, students sort the photos into two piles: living and nonliving. Then they compare with a neighboring group to see if the result was the same.

   - The history teacher asks student pairs to research one from a list of other people to determine whether or not they fit the concept of leadership: for example, Christopher Columbus, Charles Darwin, and King George III. Pairs share their findings with the class, using evidence to defend their claim that the person they researched was or was not an example of leadership.

3. **Confirm Critical Attributes:** Finally, the teacher guides students through the critical attributes of the concept. That's right, the more formal "definition" of the concept comes at the *end* of the lesson. By this time, students have a fairly solid understanding of the concept, so they actually *understand* what they're writing down and won't go home to try to *memorize* the definition like it's a fact.

4. **Reflection:** It's also nice to spend a little time reflecting at the end of the lesson. When was it that you "got" the concept? Which examples or nonexamples were most challenging for you? How did your partner/group help you develop your understanding of the concept? What makes a concept different from a fact? How is it different to learn about a concept (as opposed to a fact)?

5. **Concept Wall and Concept Maps:** It's a good idea to designate one space of the room as your concept wall—a space to put all the concepts as you study them. Students can use them to frequently draw concept maps and connections between and among different concepts at different points throughout the school year, as most concepts in every discipline are related to each other in some way.

Strategy #7: Marzano's six-step vocabulary model.

Researcher Robert Marzano (2004) identified six steps in helping students solidify their understanding of academic vocabulary. This is another way to introduce new concepts to students. The steps and a brief explanation are listed here directly from his book.

The first three steps are used to introduce a new term to students. The last three steps address different types of multiple exposures that students should experience over time to help them shape and sharpen their understanding of the terms. The six steps are as follows:

Step 1: Explain—Provide a student-friendly description, explanation, or example of the new term.

Step 2: Restate—Ask students to restate the description, explanation, or example in their own words.

Step 3: Show—Ask students to construct a picture, symbol, or graphic representation of the term.

Step 4: Discuss—Engage students periodically in structured vocabulary discussions that help them add to their knowledge of the terms in their vocabulary notebooks.

Step 5: Refine and reflect—Periodically ask students to return to their notebooks to discuss and refine entries.

Step 6: Apply in learning games—Involve students periodically in games that allow them to play with terms.

Strategy #8: SEEI presentations.

You may remember this acronym from one of the exercises outlined in Chapter 2. It's one of our favorite tools from the Foundation for Critical Thinking, and we highly recommend that you check out their miniguidebooks. This one can be found in *The Thinker's Guide to How to Write a Paragraph* (Paul & Elder, 2013). The last step of *illustrate* is especially good for building their conceptual muscle, as making a comparison in a metaphor inherently requires abstracting to the conceptual level. Using this strategy has the added impact of helping students develop strong literacy skills.

The strategy itself is incredibly simple: Give students written explanations of a key concept in all of its complexities; then ask them to teach the concept to others. This is *not* the same as asking students to copy down a definition for the concept or briefly explain it to a partner. Notice how the steps below encourage more substantive engagement with the concept and produce greater understanding.

1. Begin by finding (or writing) a clear, but complex explanation of the target concept. We find that most mathematics and science textbooks offer such explanations, as well as illustrative examples, but that teachers rarely assign them because they are difficult to understand. This activity works best when there is an element of challenge, so resist the urge to oversimplify the explanation. A one- or two-page overview with plenty of elaboration and some examples tends to work best. You could also use short video clips.

2. Assign students to small groups, and ask them to read the explanation out loud together with the goal of understanding the target concept. Encourage them to ask questions and seek answers using the resources available to them (Internet, textbooks, the teacher, etc.).

3. Once students have a basic understanding of the concept, have them work together to explain the concept in their own words using the SEEI model (see Figure 3.5). Have them write out their explanation on poster paper or by another means so it will be visible to others during their presentation. Encourage students to spend ample time crafting their explanation to make sure it is clear and precise. Circulate to provide feedback as they go. Encourage them to be creative and generate good examples, nonexamples, and illustrations of the concept. Disallow the use of examples embedded in the provided text. Students should come up with their own examples and nonexamples to demonstrate understanding.

FIGURE 3.5   SEEI MODEL

State, Elaborate, Exemplify, Illustrate (SEEI)
State the idea clearly.
Elaborate on the idea. In other words. . . . This is not to say . . . but rather . . . .
Exemplify. For example . . . . However, a nonexample would be . . . because. . . .
(Illustrate with a metaphor or image) It's like. . . .

SOURCE: Adapted from Paul, R., & Elder, L. (2013). *The thinker's guide to how to write a paragraph: The art of substantive writing.* Tomales, CA: Foundatio...

Have [...] the class. You may [...] a few groups to share their statem[...] to elaborate on it [...] provide examples. We like to have [...] their [...] since these tend to be more varied than the other [...] are often the best indicators o[...] are required to make abstract comp[...] to nonlinguistic form. Encourage the audience [...] to ask questions to gauge the presenters' understanding and elucidate meaning.

Concept-[...] Teaching in Two Words: Un[...]cover and Transfer

The [...] preceding strategies are important [...] the journey for conceptual unde[...]standing. When dealing with familiar concepts, we must first gauge students' preinstructional understanding. We must also be deliberate in how we introduce new concepts. But the crux of conceptual learning is developing deep, sophisticated understandings about conceptual *relationships*. The next chapter provides four lesson frameworks for this most important aspect of conceptual teaching, but the following two sections offer two simple ideas to help frame the process for students to develop understandings about the conceptual relationships.

A few years ago, our colleague Dave Yarmchuk made some amazing stickers to help the Concept-Based model "stick" in teachers' brains. They were oh-so-simple, but oh-so-effective. We had read H. Lynn Erickson's and Lois Lanning's books

(2014, 2017) on Concept-Based Curriculum and Instruction, and the supporting research from the National Research Council in *How Students Learn* (Donovan & Bransford, 2005), and tons of discipline-specific books about the fundamental and powerful concepts that underpin mathematics, science, history, language arts, music, and other subjects. It was complex, but he managed to capture the essence of what we were finding in two little words:

Uncover → Transfer

In these two words, his stickers summed up the most important principles of conceptual learning and helped teachers avoid the two most common pitfalls.

Step #1: Uncover. If you're a fan of *Understanding by Design*, you will recognize the term *uncoverage* from Wiggins and McTighe (2005). What does it mean? It means that instead of the teacher "covering" the content kids need to know—as in, "Jose, you should know this, we covered it on Friday!"—teachers need to plan for *students* to uncover the big ideas of the unit through inquiry.

The biggest pitfall we've seen teachers fall into with conceptual teaching is "covering" the concept by telling kids what the relationship between two concepts is. No joke, we've walked into classrooms where kids were copying notes from the board that said, "Some people hold more power in society than others." This is *not* what we mean when we say kids need to learn about the relationship between identity and power. The teacher may have "covered" power, but the kids never "uncovered" its meaning, nor did they gain any insight into the way it shapes their world. Uncoverage is key.

Step #2: Transfer. Once students uncover or discover the relationship between two or more concepts, they can use this knowledge to unlock new situations. This is the goal of conceptual learning: transfer. For instance, students in a social studies class might study ancient China and Egypt (Grade 2, Virginia Standards of Learning, 2008) to uncover the idea that "Limited resources require people to make choices about producing and consuming goods and services." This insight is a beautiful product in itself, and many teachers fall into the trap of stopping here. We've made it! Success! But understanding the relationship among concepts is just Step #1. The real reason we want students to uncover these relationships is so they begin to see their world differently. We want students to discover conceptual relationships so they can use their new knowledge to analyze problems, make decisions, and influence others in ways that matter to them.

So *after* students have uncovered a relationship, they need to practice transfer. Consider this next step: Students read articles, watch videos, or conduct interviews related to the drought in California. The teacher asks, *Knowing what you do about limited resources and consuming goods and services, how might you design an ad campaign that advocates choices about water use in California?* Students then work in groups to come up with ad campaigns that take into consideration the complexity of choices in consuming goods and services, present them to the class, and discuss how their understanding of scarcity, resources, and consuming goods and services helped influence their choices. Does this take more time? Will you cover less content? Yes, of course! Conceptual learning demands time and energy for transfer. It's not optional!

> Once students uncover or discover the relationship between two or more concepts, they can use this knowledge to unlock new situations.

Here's the tricky part about transfer: It's easy to get sucked into topical extensions rather than conceptual transfer. Topical extensions might mean teaching a unit on ancient China and Egypt and then asking students to identify ways in which these civilizations influence society today. In this case, students use their knowledge of the facts and the topic studied, but they don't actually have to use the concepts at all. It's a lovely extension activity. It probably boosts engagement. It helps kids see "real-world connections." But it's not conceptual transfer, because you're not asking them to apply insights about the conceptual relationships.

As students practice transfer to new situations, they can also practice research skills by finding their own new contexts. To keep with the same example above about ancient civilizations, an authentic transfer task would ask students to find a current example and prove that the idea about scarcity and consumer choices holds true, using evidence from both ancient China and Egypt studied in class and the current example found through research.

Also notice that a transfer task makes a meaningful performance assessment for conceptual understanding. There's no way for students to succeed in this task by simply memorizing something the teacher said in class. You'll see right away if they don't understand the concepts or if their ability to apply them is weak. When you give them something new and ask them to show you how their understanding of the concepts helps them problem-solve, there's no faking. They'll know it, and you'll know it.

Strategy #9: Learning as uncovering and transferring understanding.

Show the image below to students and discuss the following questions:

- What do the keys represent in a Concept-Based classroom? *The conceptual relationships.*
- Why are they buried underground? *Because the students must uncover them through specific contexts.*
- What does the treasure chest represent? *A new or novel situation they can unlock with their conceptual understanding.*
- Who is doing the uncovering? *The learner and not the teacher.*

FIGURE 3.6   UNCOVER AND TRANSFER

SOURCE: Jimmy Conde, graphic artist

The best part about these two principles—uncover and transfer—is that they put the burden of thinking on the student. This is key for maximizing learning.

Uncover: The Conceptual Inquiry Cycle

Again, the most important point to remember for conceptual learning is that the students **uncover** the conceptual relationships and express their unique understanding of these relationships in their own words. That is why the guiding questions and the art of crafting them are so important. This way of teaching is typically called inquiry-based, inductive, or constructivist teaching. It is the best method for deep understanding, because the students make meaning for themselves.

Strategy #10: The conceptual inquiry cycle.

FIGURE 3.7   ~~CONCEPTUAL INQUIRY~~ CYCLE   *LEARNING TRANSFER*

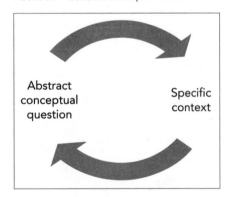

Abstract conceptual question

Specific context

SOURCE: © 2015 Julie Stern

At a very basic level, instruction should cycle frequently through two major components (see Figure 3.7):

- Students respond to abstract questions of conceptual relationship.

- Students explore a specific context—a mathematical problem, scientific experiment, historical moment, or passage of text—in which the concepts play a major role.

1. Pose a conceptual question to students, and then take them through a specific context that illustrates the relationship. In other words, the context helps to answer the abstract conceptual question.

TOOLS FOR TEACHING CONCEPTUAL UNDERSTANDING, ELEMENTARY

2. After careful study of the specific context, students reconsider the conceptual question in light of the information studied. Specific contexts provide the foundation for understanding the more abstract conceptual relationship, and the concepts help students gain insight into the specific contexts studied. **The facts and examples studied in the new context become the evidence to support their generalization about the concepts**. Students must provide **evidence** to illustrate the statements of conceptual relationship; this is essential.

3. The next step is to provide a second context to further illustrate the relationship between the concepts. The more contexts or facts students collect, the deeper their understanding and the more sophisticated their ability is to apply it to new situations. By studying the same conceptual question in many different contexts, we are able to balance depth of learning with breadth of learning. The breadth comes from the variety of contexts and examples to which students are exposed. However, unlike coverage-centered classrooms, the Concept-Based classroom also achieves a depth of understanding by filtering the many contexts through the concepts of the unit.

What does this look like in a classroom? Consider the example in Figure 3.8.

Students study the relationship between animals' characteristics and their environments. They may begin with the simplest or clearest example and move on to progressively more complex examples to deepen and complicate their understanding as the unit goes on. For example, a unit on adaptation might begin with animals who simply migrate when the environment becomes too cold. But then students could look at other animals who have characteristics that allow them to survive in the cold. In the end, they have gained knowledge of whales, chameleons, camels, and bats. More important, though, they have used their study of these topics to uncover a deep, enduring understanding about ways in which animals adapt in response to their environment. This is much more interesting and useful to students than a unit that "covers" all of these topics but does not bring conceptual coherence to the learning.

FIGURE 3.8 DEEPER LEARNING

Real classroom example: Adaptations

Conceptual question: What is the relationship between characteristics of animals and their environment?

Contexts:

- Introductory context: whales and other animals that migrate to warmer waters
- Chameleons that change color
- Camels in the desert
- Bats and other nocturnal creatures

In a nutshell, **we first pose an interesting question about the nature of a conceptual relationship for students to answer.** This allows the students and the teacher to become aware of any preconceptions, prior knowledge, and misunderstandings. Then, students explore the concepts in a specific context (a factual example, text, or other slice of content) that allows them to abstract back up to answer the question. The context is chosen carefully to enable discovery of the answer to the conceptual question. The students' responses to the conceptual question in light of the facts of the specific context serve as the evidence of understanding (or not) and are the most important part.

The introductory context needs more direction and guidance from the teacher. Early on, the teacher may provide guiding questions to lead students to a specific insight or may present the context in a way that highlights the concepts at play. Texts, videos, or class activities should be designed to lead students down a fairly straightforward path of understanding. The goal is convergent, meaning that the teacher wants all students to uncover (roughly) the same conceptual relationship here.

As students deepen their understanding by applying the conceptual relationship to new contexts, their need for these teacher supports diminishes. Now, instead of pushing students toward a certain understanding of the conceptual relationship, the teacher begins to challenge and complicate the understandings that students are coming to. At this point the goal can be divergent, meaning that students can uncover unique conceptual relationships, perhaps even arriving at conclusions that contradict those of their peers, for extremely deep learning. Of course, all generalizations must be accompanied by strong evidence from the contexts.

You may notice that the conceptual inquiry process is iterative. By this we mean that students should study the same conceptual relationship as it appears in several different contexts. When studying English, this might mean that students return to the conceptual question after reading one of Aesop's fables, with each fable serving as a separate context. Another option would be to pair Aesop's fables with Grimms' fairy tales, studying the same concepts in the context of two different series of short stories. In mathematics, these contexts may be a series of problems that escalate in complexity. In any case, **it is essential that students stop to explicitly reconsider their understanding of the conceptual relationship by returning to the conceptual question several times throughout the unit of study, not just at the end.**

This brings us to an essential part of uncovering the relationship among the concepts: refining and increasing the sophistication of students' ideas. Remember that we always begin with students' preconceptions about the concepts. Often, students already know quite a bit about the concepts from their prior learning and personal experience. It is not enough for students to go through the motions of the unit, allowing their ideas to remain static. Students must show their learning by tracing the evolution of their thinking as they make their ideas clearer, more precise, more logical, and more sophisticated. This is another key component for achieving deeper learning.

Strategy #11: Generate, sort, connect, elaborate.

Another excellent strategy from *Making Thinking Visible: How to Promote Engagement, Understanding, and Independence for All Learners* (Ritchhart et al., 2011) really helps to scaffold students arriving at their own statements of conceptual relationship. Below is the explanation:

Select a topic, concept, or issue for which you want to map your understanding.

- **Generate** a list of ideas and initial thoughts that come to mind when you think about this topic or issue.
- **Sort** your ideas according to how central or tangential they are. Place central ideas near the center and more tangential ideas toward the outside of the page.
- **Connect** your ideas by drawing connecting lines between the ideas that have something in common. Write a short sentence explaining how the ideas are connected.
- **Elaborate** on any of the ideas or thoughts you have written so far by adding new ideas that expand, extend, or add to your initial ideas. (p. 125)

For younger students to understand this process, we find it useful to start by modeling the process using very familiar things, such as "pencil, homework, desk." Then we move to something they can use to practice, such as "football, grass, people, rules." We also find it helpful to do the first stage for them by giving them the words we would like them to sort and connect. Use the words *most important* as part of sorting, or you can skip that step and just ask them how two or more ideas are connected. We also often skip the last step until students have practiced it a few times—but inevitably they will start to come up with related ideas on their own!

Strategy #12: Comparing surface and deep learning.

As students move through the conceptual inquiry cycle, be sure to remind them of the process and goal of iterative learning. Consider showing them the visual in Figure 3.9, and ask them to compare the two swimmers. What are the implications? Students should come up with ideas such as these: The deeper the diver goes, the more interesting the ocean becomes. Or if we only stay at the surface, learning can

FIGURE 3.9   SURFACE VERSUS DEEP LEARNING

SOURCE: Jimmy Conde, graphic artist

be quite boring. Each new context students study should take them deeper, helping their generalizations become more interesting, insightful, and well supported.

Transfer Is Both a Means and an End

It can sometimes be confusing to say that the goal of conceptual learning is transfer. When teachers hear this, they often think that this means transfer comes at the end of a unit. We often hear teachers say, *This is great! I teach students about the concepts for a few weeks, and then I design an assessment where they have to apply their understanding to a new situation. If they can transfer the idea, we've hit our goal!*

This isn't quite right. If we wait until the end of a unit of study to give students the chance to transfer their understanding to a new situation, we're bound to be disappointed. Students need regular and frequent practice testing out their generalizations and determining how they apply in a new context.

The beauty of teaching through the inquiry cycle, following an iterative process where students investigate the concepts over and over again in new ways, is that it's easy to offer transfer opportunities throughout the unit. Think about it. Students begin with an idea about the relationship between two concepts based on their prior knowledge. Then they test this understanding in a new context during the first inquiry cycle. They're transferring already!

The tricky part is that students are not naturally good at transferring their understanding. Although our brains are wired to draw out conceptual relationships from a set of examples—think of the toddler who learns early on that green vegetables taste bad—we rarely execute this process consciously. Additionally, by the time students reach secondary school, they have often stopped expecting school to make sense or have any practical application. Because of this, they need help to become conscious of and deliberately execute the process for conceptual transfer:

1. **Recognize the concepts that apply:** Which concepts are at work in this situation? Which conceptual relationships seem to be shaping this scenario?

2. **Engage prior understanding of the conceptual relationship:** What do I already know to be true about the relationship among these concepts? What specific examples support my understanding?

3. **Determine the extent to which prior understanding applies:** What makes this new situation different from the situations I've studied in the past? Is my generalization likely to hold true in this situation? Which parts of my prior understanding transfer and which don't?

4. **Modify and refine understanding based on the new situation:** How can I reshape my understanding in light of this new situation?

Students often want learning to be black and white. Contradictions and complications are generally unwelcome, and their brains work to sift them out. But a significant understanding of any conceptual relationship requires students to face, and directly deal with, examples and information that don't fit the generalizations they've built. This means that generalizations cannot always be applied wholesale to every new situation, and that it is important to pay close attention to what makes a new situation unique.

Here's an example of what we mean. When learning about the ways people lived in the past, students often conclude that people's customs and ways of living change over time.

They may look at the United States during the Colonial Period, Civil War, Jazz Age, and Great Depression as separate contexts. In every case, technology and other factors influence and change the way people live. But then they may look at a celebration such as the Fourth of July and see a different story all together. Americans have been celebrating with parades and fireworks for many generations. This helps them to see that although ways of living tend to change over time, there are some traditions and customs that remain quite the same.

This is why transfer is so important in deepening and refining their understanding. Transfer can help students unlock new situations by recognizing familiar patterns. At the same time, though, mindless transfer can lead students to misunderstand new phenomena by erasing the unique features at hand.

> Transfer can help students unlock new situations by recognizing familiar patterns. At the same time, though, mindless transfer can lead students to misunderstand new phenomena by erasing the unique features at hand.

It is important, then, that teachers design opportunities for students to not just practice transfer, but to "fail" at transfer. This means they need to interact with situations where their generalizations will not hold completely true and may even get in the way. Strategy #13 offers one way to do this.

Strategy #13: Transfer and its limitations.

Consider incorporating this activity into the middle or end of any unit of study. It is important that students have thought about the concepts and have formed some generalizations prior to this activity.

1. Discuss the meaning of transfer with students. This term can get cloudy, so we find it helpful to talk about three aspects of transfer:

   - **Analysis:** Transferring understanding means you can break a new situation down into its component parts according to predictable patterns. (Example: mathematics students can determine patterns by recognizing the relationship between even numbers, odd numbers, and addition.)

   - **Making predictions:** Transferring understanding means you can predict the likely outcome or impact of a new situation. (Example: Science students anticipate that a decline in bee population will cause major consequences for other species living in the same habitat.)

   - **Solving a problem:** Transferring understanding means you can come up with solutions to a problem based on your understanding of the concepts. (Example: Geography students can offer measures to prevent conflicts over resources based on a deep understanding of how resources and conflict are related.)

2. Ask students to generate a list of ways they could transfer their understanding of the concepts currently being studied. Ask them to think of at least one way they could use their understanding to analyze a new situation, make predictions, or create solutions. Discuss their lists, noting the ways in which transfer is useful.

3. Next, offer students a scenario where their understanding of the concepts is sure to fall short. This will vary by discipline and unit, but the following list of options may help you identify a good example:

   - A mathematical problem of a different type

   - An anomaly or exception

   - An example that shares some obvious characteristics with previous contexts studied, but deep down is very different

4. Ask students to analyze, make predictions, or offer solutions based on their conceptual understanding. Then discuss the accuracy of their application. For instance, if students are making predictions, reveal the actual outcome of the situation. Discuss the following questions:

   - What made it difficult to predict how well your understanding would transfer to this context?

   - What clues in the new context might have signaled to you that your generalization would not apply easily to the situation?

   - What is the danger of mindlessly transferring your understanding without considering the differences of each individual context or situation?

Sample Instructional Calendar

Most schools use two common written curriculum documents: unit planners outlining the goals of the unit and usually the summative assessment, and daily lesson planners. At the risk of adding to the long list of things teachers must produce, we advocate the use of a simple calendar that at least roughly sketches out the sequence of lessons and learning experiences. It's not etched in stone, as we must respond to the learning needs of the students. But it provides guidance to ensure we will have enough time for all of the learning goals.

And at the risk of the reader thinking we advocate one discrete way of doing this—*which we don't*—we've included a sample unit calendar to illustrate how one might approach sequencing lessons in a Concept-Based classroom. Figure 3.10 shows a sample unit general calendar that can be adapted to any unit.

This sample unit calendar is from a third-grade unit on sustainability and is meant to help you visualize how you might plan out a sequence of lessons for a Concept-Based unit—but it is only one example of a million ways to organize instruction. We only attempt to illustrate how you might start with an abstract conceptual question and take students through the conceptual inquiry cycle multiple times before the summative assessment. Chapter 4 outlines five instructional frameworks that will add more details about exactly what each step of that cycle can look like.

Balancing Conceptual Thinking, Skills Practice, Memorization, and Review

Many teachers worry about the amount of time that instruction for conceptual understanding takes, especially compared with traditional instruction. We used to think that the depth of study into a concept and corresponding topics inevitably meant that we had to spend more time with fewer topics, which was scary. But the better we got at teaching this way, we realized students learn *more* factual content because they actually remember what they've learned and are able to make insightful connections throughout the year demonstrating a depth of understanding.

In fact, we were forced to confront the **myth** that so many of us hold dear: *If we cover material (e.g., tell students something or go over it in class), they will learn it.* This is something many teachers are convinced is true despite so much evidence to the contrary. It may feel more efficient in the short term to spoon-feed students with information or explain step-by-step how to do something. But when they lack depth of understanding, they either repeat incorrectly, repeat partially, or forget. Anyone teaching for longer than two

> When students lack depth of understanding, they either repeat incorrectly, repeat partially, or forget.

FIGURE 3.10 SAMPLE UNIT CALENDAR

Lessons 1–2

- Initial thinking concept-map of sustainability
- Sustainability images: see, think, wonder
- Concept attainment activity on sustainability with common attributes and examples

Lessons 3–4

- Abstract conceptual question with initial responses: What is the relationship between humans and sustainability?
- Discuss additional concepts of the unit and start a concept wall
- Possible investigations: food, water, transportation, electricity

What is the relationship between humans and sustainability?

Specific context

Lessons 5–6

- Context 1: human needs
- Jigsaw food, water, transportation, and electricity
- Refine responses to question

What is the relationship between humans and sustainability?

Specific context

Lessons 7–8

- Context 2: types of energy-producing resources
- Graphic organizer on finite to infinite scale and impact on the planet
- Refine responses again

What is the relationship between humans and sustainability?

Specific context

Lessons 9–10

- Context 3: human actions
- Guest speaker on carbon footprint and responsible behavior
- Refine responses again

What is the relationship between humans and sustainability?

Specific context

Lessons 11–12

- Generate-sort-connect-elaborate
- Sustainable farm visit
- Refine responses again

Lessons 13–14

- Summarize all responses and document how thinking has improved.
- I used to think . . . but then. . . . Now I think . . . .
- Present our work to an authentic audience

Summative Task

- Analyze the proposed Keystone Pipeline and discuss the balance between human needs and sustainability in this situation. Propose a solution that uses evidence from our study.

What is the relationship between humans and sustainability?

Specific context

months has seen this. Two lessons later, one week later, one month later, the following school year—we are repeatedly shocked by what students either misunderstand, partially understand, or forget.

Consider the metaphors explained in this short excerpt from the *The Art of Redesigning Instruction* by Paul (n.d.) from the Foundation for Critical Thinking:

> When we teach in "mother robin" fashion—trying to mentally chew up everything for our students so we can put it into their intellectual beaks to swallow—students tend to become, if I can slightly mix my metaphor, "Polly parrot" learners: "I can't understand anything unless you tell me exactly how and what to say and think. I need you to figure out everything for me. I shouldn't have to do more than repeat what you or the textbook say."

Unfortunately, the more students grow in this direction, the more teachers try to amplify their mother robin teaching to accommodate it. Growth on either side produces a compensating growth on the other. By the middle school level, most students are deeply entrenched in learning—and teachers in teaching—nothing but lower-order, fragmented, surface knowledge. Teachers feel by this level that they have no choice but to think for their students, or worse, that they should not require any thinking at all, that students are not really capable of it.

We love this article, and suggest reading it in its entirety. It reminds us that our solution to the problem of chronic forgetting—more review, more discrete practice, more work to "break it down" for students—often only makes the problem worse—not to mention the time that is wasted in doing this!

Let us say this: research—and all of our experience—says that if students deeply understand the conceptual relationships of an academic discipline, they will retain facts better and be able to transfer what they've learned (Bransford, 2000; Bruner, 1977; Hattie, 2012; Newmann, Bryk, & Nagaoka, 2001). If they don't deeply understand, they will forget and need to be retaught again and again, year after year. Most teachers think about their course in isolation. Many do not realize the incredible amount of repetition that happens year after year in almost all of the subject areas, especially language arts and mathematics. In a topic-based, coverage-centered teaching model, the results are plain and simple: Students forget. It's as if they go home at night, lie down, and everything falls out of their ears and onto the floor!

When it comes to skill building that is fundamental as children are learning to read and write, we argue that Concept-Based Curriculum and Instruction is still an incredibly useful way to plan units. Consider the following conceptual understanding for kindergarten or first grade: *We use language in formal and informal ways.* We could ask students, *What are the different ways we use language? Why do we use language in different ways?* And we could have them compare the ways in which we talk to our friends, babies, or dolls with the ways of talking in news reports, safety information, and stories, all serving as different contexts on the conceptual inquiry cycle. This could be followed with an understanding such as, *Formal language has rules and structures to help us communicate clearly* to extend learning and give students the "why" behind grammar rules.

When planning for skill instruction, please refer to Lois Lanning's structure of process as shown in Figure 1.6 in Chapter 1. Using her model, try to come up with the big idea or the "why" behind the complex process associated with the strategy or skill. Then, following our model, present students with an abstract conceptual question along with specific contexts that illuminate the answer, helping students to discover the "why" behind the complex process.

Of course, there is a need for skills practice and memorization to the point of automaticity. Balance is important, and it is wise to spend some time each week to develop students' memory and speed at recall of important facts or basic skills. As a general practice, it makes sense to allow time for this *after* we have hooked students with an interesting conceptual question, conducted a concept-attainment lesson, and explored at least one interesting context of the abstract conceptual question at play in factual content. In general, we like to repeat the following mantra to ourselves: understanding first, drills for automaticity second.

If you are worried about how parents might react to a shift in teaching and learning, we recommend sharing Erickson and Lanning's (2014) Structure of Knowledge and Structure of Process, as well as some of the research presented here, to help them understand why we are teaching in ways that might be different from the learning experiences of their childhood. We have told them that there are two reasons why a conceptual approach is imperative:

1.   The research shows it helps students to *retain* information better than memorization alone by building conceptual schema in their brains.
2.   It also helps students to *transfer* their understanding to unique and new situations by giving students abstract ideas that will unlock complex situations.

Conclusion

In this chapter we've offered some strategies to help teachers design lesson segments that align with conceptual learning goals. But we hope our readers understand that these strategies are just a starting point to help them envision the many possible ways that students can experience conceptual learning. More important than the individual strategies are the underlying principles outlined at the start of the chapter. They are worth repeating:

1. We need to expose students' **preinstructional understanding** of the concepts and conceptual relationship.

2. A deep understanding of **each concept by itself** is necessary for a sophisticated understanding of the relationship among several concepts.

3. Students must **uncover** the conceptual relationship for themselves.

4. Transfer is both a means to and an end of conceptual learning.

Teachers who understand these principles can easily improvise beyond the strategies provided here to meet the needs of their particular students in a way that suits their preferred teaching style. In Chapter 4 we'll show you how to combine these strategies and sequence lesson components to create dynamic, cohesive learning paths for a variety of unit types.

Chapter Review

- Why is it important to engage students' prior understanding of the concepts at the start of a unit or lesson? What strategies might you employ to do this?

- What can teachers do to develop understanding—not memorization—of new concepts early in a unit of study?

- What is the meaning of the phrase "Uncover and Transfer"? What do these steps look like in the classroom?

- What is the relationship between transfer of learning and deep learning?

CHAPTER 4

What Additional Tools Can We Use to Design Lessons?

We've adapted five popular instructional models to further guide the planning process and to ensure students **uncover conceptual relationships**. The most important thing to remember when adapting any instructional tool is to make certain that conceptual understanding is the goal.

Each of these well-liked models has great features aimed to engage students and foster learning that lasts. They are sometimes implemented, however, with the same surface level of understanding as traditional teaching methods. The first step in designing lessons is always identifying the statement of conceptual relationship that represents one of the goals of the unit.

> The most important thing to remember when adapting any instructional tool is to make certain that conceptual understanding is the goal.

The four major steps in any Concept-Based lesson framework are as follows:

1. Students respond with initial thoughts to **conceptual questions** about the relationship between the concepts.

2. Students explore one or more **specific contexts** that illustrate the nature of the relationship and give students the fact base needed for deep thinking.

3. Students **explain (write, draw, tell, etc.) a statement of conceptual relationship** with evidence from the context to help support and explain the relationship.

4. Students **transfer** their understanding to a new situation.

All of the lesson frameworks in this chapter follow the basic steps above with a few additions added in between the steps. Each framework contains a list of steps with corresponding questions to spur thought and a few examples of what it might look like in action. It is extremely important to note that the steps most often occur over multiple class periods, especially when classes are about an hour.

Lesson Framework #1: The Inquiry Process

The inquiry process is perhaps the most popular instructional model in elementary schools. Although there is no common definition of what is meant by *inquiry*, nearly all approaches we've seen have student-centered investigation at the core of learning. Teachers aim to help students develop their own questions and pursue investigations according to their particular interests. It can be a very difficult teaching model to pull off, especially with larger class sizes.

Concept-Based Instruction uses either structured or guided inquiry, as the teacher has conceptual understandings as the goals of the unit (Erickson et al., 2017). We've adapted some of the steps from Kathy Short's Authoring Cycle (Carber & Davidson, 2010) for inquiry into a process for conceptual understanding. See Figure 4.1 for a list of lesson steps, question stems, and what this process might look like in the classroom.

Let's look at an example unit on migration, culture, and tradition (Texas Essential Knowledge and Skills for Social Studies, Grade 2). Two of the conceptual goals of the unit might be these:

- People migrate to meet a variety of needs.
- Migrants bring customs and traditions, which often contribute to changes in the community.

For the connecting and exploring phase, students could work in small groups to draw what comes to mind when they hear the words *custom* or *tradition*. Next, teachers could transform each of the second-grade classrooms with images, music, clothing, and artifacts from different immigrant groups who came to Houston. Classes rotate through each room and collect evidence using a graphic organizer to draw or write different things that they see.

In the second phase, teachers could explain that students are going to learn about the concept of human migration. They could do a concept attainment activity where students explore images and examples of migration to determine common attributes. Next, teachers could ask students to brainstorm as many questions as possible that they might have about migration, and then teachers could help students to sort and rank the questions and select the ones they will explore. Each group should look for reasons why the group migrated and for evidence of customs or traditions they brought with them.

FIGURE 4.1   THE INQUIRY PROCESS LESSON FRAMEWORK

Lesson Step	Question Stems	Might Look Like
1. Connecting and Exploring Stimulus/Hook: The "why" of the unit. We want to generate interest and connect to prior knowledge by having students ask, Why is this topic important to me? What do I already think about it? The question stems are written in third person, because this is usually teacher-led. We want to connect to their prior knowledge and their lives while stimulating interest in the unit.	• Imagine _____. • What might happen if _____. • How is this important? • Is this true: _____? • Which is more important: _____ or ____? • What comes to mind when you think of/hear the word _____? • What do you like about _____? • How often do you rely on _____? • Why is _____ important to you, your family, our community, our city?	• Images • Skits • Touching/tactile objects • Music/art • Transform the classroom • Videos • Sample food/smells • Learning walk • Students drawing their ideas
2. Asking Questions This part shifts to being more student-directed but with **clear teacher goals** about the big ideas (conceptual relationships) that we want the students to "uncover" via exploration and research.	• What are the concepts of this unit? • Which relationships should we investigate? • What impacts should we investigate? • What questions might we ask? • How should we investigate this? • What do we want to find out? • What do we need to know first, second, third? • What can we compare or contrast this to? • What is our research question? • What is our hypothesis?	• Teacher models coming up with questions. • Guest scientists and other adults model coming up with questions. • Give students choice of example questions. • Brainstorm as many questions as possible; then sort them. • Rank a set of questions. • Rank a set of hypotheses. • Rank a set of possible investigations.

(Continued)

FIGURE 4.1   (Continued)

Lesson Step	Question Stems	Might Look Like
	• What patterns might we notice? • What examples will help us to understand this better?	• Concept attainment activity. • Rank a set of possible methods of investigation.
3. Investigating and Organizing This is the real substance of the unit. We must carefully facilitate student discovery of the *relationship* between concepts to gain greater insight into a topic.	• What evidence can I collect about the relationships between concepts? • What patterns do I notice? • What effects do I notice? • What further questions do I have as a result of my investigation? • How will we show what we learned?	• Graphic organizers • Concept maps • Cause/effect diagrams • Compare/contrast diagrams • Explicit teaching of research strategies and tools • Visible thinking routines • At least one transfer of understanding to a new situation
4. Going Further This is where we give a summative assessment of learning via a new situation or context that ideally involves a real-life, important issue to unpack. We also want students to take action in some way to make learning authentic and purposeful.	• How has my understanding deepened as a result of my investigation? • How can I apply my understanding to a new situation? • What slight differences can I find in the new situation, and how does that deepen my understanding? • How can I take action on this topic?	• GRASP (goal, role, audience, situation, public product) • Presentation to authentic audience • At least second transfer • Reflection on how the unit changed them as a person and how they are going to make a difference

Once students begin investigating and organizing, they could choose a particular group that migrated to Houston to research. Teachers could first teach explicit research strategies and then provide resources for students to conduct guided research into their selected group. Using graphic organizers, students could create a product to showcase what they've learned to their classmates.

In the final phase, students could perhaps create a mural on a school wall depicting the different groups and cultures that make up the Houston community and reveal it during a parent–teacher association meeting. During the meeting, they could conduct an oral reflection for a parent on how they grew as learners during the course of the unit. For the summative assessment, they could learn about a group not yet studied and explain how that group made an impact on the cultures and traditions of Houston.

Lesson Framework #2: Generating and Testing Hypotheses

Once students have been introduced to the concepts that anchor your unit of study, they are ready to generate and test hypotheses about the relationships among those concepts. In his book *The Art and Science of Teaching* (2007), Robert Marzano notes that providing opportunities for students to generate hypotheses and test them—through experimental inquiry, problem solving, decision making, or investigation tasks—has been proven to produce substantial learning gains. This is likely because the process of generating and testing hypotheses engages students' preconceptions about the concepts (their initial hypotheses will reveal their preconceptions about how the concepts relate to each other) and asks them to become aware of the ways in which new knowledge challenges or confirms their prior understanding.

Generating and testing hypotheses about conceptual relationships generally happens through these steps:

1. Students write initial response to conceptual questions (their preconceptions).

2. Students learn a little about a specific context, enough to generate a hypothesis (topic/context/facts).

3. Students develop a hypothesis about the conceptual relationship in light of the topic.

4. Students learn more about the topic in order to test their hypotheses.

5. Students abstract to an improved statement of conceptual relationship supported by evidence from the context. (Steps 4 and 5 can be repeated several times.)

6. Students transfer this understanding to a new situation.

7. Students reflect on growth in thinking and understanding.

To prepare to take their students through these steps, teachers can follow the framework shown in Figure 4.2.

As an example, let's look at a fourth-grade lesson on poetry. The conceptual relationship might be something like, *Poets use rhyme and repeated line to establish the mood of a poem.*

1. **Conceptual question:** Students record initial responses to the question: Why do poets use rhymes and repeated lines?

2. **Background:** Next they learn a little about the poet Cristina Rossi and that they are going to read a poem called "Who Has Seen the Wind?"

FIGURE 4.2   GENERATING AND TESTING HYPOTHESES LESSON FRAMEWORK

Lesson Principle	Questions to Ask Yourself	Might Look Like
1. Start with **conceptual questions** that target the statement of conceptual relationships of the unit.	• What conceptual relationships are at the heart of this unit? • How can I create conceptual questions that engage students and allow for deep thought right away? • What questions will allow me to gauge students' preinstructional understanding of the concepts?	• Students recording initial thoughts about conceptual relationships in journal. • Groups draw nonlinguistic representations of the concept on chart paper and gallery walk to see breadth of class's thinking. • Small groups discuss conceptual questions and teacher observes. • Teacher provides variety of sample relationship statements, and students explain which one aligns with their thinking and why.
2. Provide enough **background** on topic of inquiry to make a hypothesis (e.g., background on author or text, preview of historical example).	• In what context will students investigate the concepts? • What background information would allow students to generate useful hypotheses about the concept in this context? • How could I preview the topic in a way that intrigues students and sets the stage for inquiry? How can I set up a "mystery" for students to solve?	• Stations or gallery walk of intriguing images that introduce basics of topic. • Short lecture or student presentation explaining basic background. • Dramatic read-aloud of key passage of text or quote about the historical event/figure. • Students read "fact sheet" with four or five key details. • Students brainstorm background knowledge in KWL (know, want to know, learned) chart.
3. Students **generate hypotheses** about the topic/text based on current understanding of conceptual relationships.	• How can students use their current understanding of the concepts to generate hypotheses about the topic/text?	• Students brainstorm hypotheses about the topic/text on sticky notes and categorize them as a group. • Students list as many hypotheses as possible in journal, and then circle the best one. • Pairs discuss and come to consensus on a hypothesis they will test together.

Lesson Principle	Questions to Ask Yourself	Might Look Like
4. Provide texts/experiences that allow students to **test their hypotheses** about the topic through a specific context.	• What experiences would allow students to test their hypotheses and gain a more nuanced or sophisticated understanding of the relationship between concepts? • Which inquiry strategies will best help students test their hypotheses about this topic?	• Individual reading, marking text for evidence for/against hypothesis, group discussion of text and evidence found. • Whole class watches video or lecture and records evidence for/against hypothesis; pairs discuss viability of hypothesis and revise if necessary. • Students research information online and collect evidence for/against hypothesis. • Students rotate through stations and gather evidence to test hypothesis.
5. Ask students to **generalize about the concepts** in light of what they learned about the topic.	• How could students use their learning about the topic to create a transferable understanding about the concepts in general?	• **Students write statements to express relationship between concepts.** • Additionally, _____. • Students draw nonlinguistic representations of the conceptual relationship and explain their thinking to a partner. • Synectics—students consider a variety of images and choose which one best represents the conceptual relationship.
6. Have students **refine and test their statements of conceptual relationship** (and peers' statements).	• How can students increase the clarity, accuracy, precision, depth, breadth, relevance, significance, and fairness of their statements? • How can students use facts to support their statements?	• Students ask "Why?" "How?" and "So what?" to improve precision and significance of statements. • Students list facts and examples *outside the context studied* that support their generalizations. • Students read others' statements and refine or support them with evidence. • Students create Structure of Knowledge diagrams to show how they built their statement. • Students perform research to further test and refine their statements.

(Continued)

FIGURE 4.2 (Continued)

Lesson Principle	Questions to Ask Yourself	Might Look Like
7. Ask students to **reflect** on learning and explain transferability of their statements of conceptual relationships.	• How can students gain awareness of their learning and the usefulness of their new understanding of the concepts? • How can I help students track their own growth in thinking and understanding?	• Students return to original thoughts about concept and compare to their new thoughts. • Students complete exit slip describing how their understanding has changed. • Students track growth on novice to expert scale/rubric (see Chapter 5) and explain what happened in their brains to make this progress. • Students name the points of the lesson when they were doing "complex" or "deep" thinking and explain what this felt like. • Pairs brainstorm situations when they could use their new idea (transferability). • Students explain how partner helped them push their thinking or led them to a breakthrough.

3. **Generate hypothesis:** Based on what they know about the poet and the name of the poem, students hypothesize about how and why the poet will use rhyme and repeated lines.

4. **Test the hypothesis:** The students read the poem and discuss what surprised them followed by the effects that rhyme and repeated lines had on the poem. Through guided discussion, the teacher could ask students about how they feel when reading the poem to elicit ideas about emotion and mood.

5. **Generalize:** Students return to the initial question with refined thinking about why poets use rhyme and repeated lines. They use evidence from the poem to defend their responses.

6. **Transfer:** Students transfer their understanding to a new poem such as "At the Zoo" by William Makepeace Thackeray. This poem is a complete change in mood and uses rhyme and repeated lines in a different way. Students discuss and then return to their refined thinking for further reflection using evidence from this new poem.

7. **Reflect:** Students reflect on the ways in which their thinking became more precise through the lesson.

Lesson Framework #3: The Workshop Model for Complex Processes

The workshop model has been common practice for English language arts classrooms for many years. It has more recently made its way into math classrooms. The idea is to provide as much classroom time as possible to students practicing skills for complex processes while the teacher provides feedback. It is not too different from the idea behind "flipped classrooms"—where students watch videos of their teacher demonstrating a skill at home and then come to school and practice it where the teacher can provide feedback. The flip is between where students receive explanation (at home) and where they practice (at school). With the workshop model, the teacher provides a minilesson at the start of class, and then the rest of the class time is for practicing the strategy presented in the minilesson.

One of the greatest proponents of the workshop model is literacy expert Chris Tovani (2011). She says,

> Just like athletes on the field who do the majority of the work during practice, students in my classroom do the majority of the work by reading, writing and thinking during class. By organizing my time using the workshop model every day, all year long, I can ensure that their reading, writing and thinking are getting better. (p. 39)

This is a particularly effective way to design lessons for subjects that are process oriented, such as the arts and languages. See Figure 1.6 in Chapter 1 for a review of the Structure of Process. While mathematics has important processes, strategies, and skills, it is essential that lessons on the knowledge side complement the process side. This cannot be the only lesson design structure used in mathematics classes. Other disciplines such as science and social studies can use this model for their statements of conceptual relationship that are from the Structure of Process. They are the complex processes that disciplinarians *do* to carry out the discipline. See Figure 4.3 for a science example.

FIGURE 4.3   SCIENCE COMPLEX PROCESS EXAMPLE

Scientists ask questions, make observations and gather information about a situation to solve problems (adapted from NGSS, K-2, ETS-1-1, Engineering Design).

The idea is to provide a minilesson on one specific strategy or skill that is essential to carrying out a complex process. For example, if the complex process is *persuasive writing*, you might focus first on *making a strong claim* and do a minilesson on just that part of persuasive writing first. Next you would allow students to practice that skill first before introducing, say, how to *use strong reasoning* and *provide relevant evidence*.

Each of those aspects of persuasive writing would be broken down into distinct lessons or a few lessons before moving on.

The purpose of calling it a minilesson means that it is both specific and brief. Students then use the remaining class time, which should be the majority of the lesson, to practice this skill or strategy. The majority of class time is dedicated to student practice and allows time for the teacher to provide specific, positive feedback. Figure 4.4 provides useful planning steps to prepare a lesson.

FIGURE 4.4   WORKSHOP MODEL LESSON FRAMEWORK

Lesson Principle	Questions to Ask Yourself	Might Look Like
1. Opening: Conceptual Questions	• What conceptual relationships are at the heart of this unit? • How can I create conceptual questions that engage students and allow for deep thought right away? • What questions will allow me to gauge students' preinstructional understanding of the concepts? • How can students connect the current goal to previous learning? • How can students use their current understanding of the concepts to connect to the day's goal? • How can students articulate the connection between the day's strategy and the overall complex process?	• Students record initial thoughts about conceptual relationships in journal. • Groups draw nonlinguistic representations of the concept on chart paper and gallery walk to see breadth of class's thinking. • Small groups discuss conceptual questions, and teacher observes. • Teacher provides variety of sample relationship statements, and students explain which one aligns with their thinking and why. • Pairs discuss and come to consensus on how today's goal links to their previous learning.
2. Minilesson	• How can I model the specific strategy or skill in a way that will clearly illustrate the *thinking moves* for this strategy or skill? • How will students engage right away with the demonstration?	• Teacher conducts a "think-aloud" to demonstrate what he or she is thinking about while executing the strategy or skill. • Students interview teacher to find out more about how he or she completes this strategy. • Students pair-share what they noticed during the demonstration.

Lesson Principle	Questions to Ask Yourself	Might Look Like
	• How will students link the demonstration to the day's work? • How will students link the minilesson to the overall complex process?	• Students watch a video that introduces a new strategy or skills for a complex process. • Students write out an explanation of how to do it in their own words; teacher circulates and corrects any errors.
3. Work time	• How will students practice the strategy or skill? • What specific context(s) will we use to allow for practice? • How will I provide guidance and feedback as they practice? • How will we celebrate success and progress made?	• Students evaluate an example of this strategy or skill. • Students practice and then evaluate their own work. • Peers give each other feedback on their practice work. • Students choose how they will practice the skill or strategy.
4. Generalize and Debrief	• How can students connect the current goal to previous learning? • How can students use their learning about the specific skill or strategy to write transferable statements of conceptual relationship about the complex process?	• Students explain how today's goal relates to the complex process. • Students write statements about the relationship between today's concept and yesterday's concept.
5. Transfer	• How can students evaluate the transferability of their statements of conceptual relationship?	• Pairs brainstorm situations when they could use their new idea (transferability). • Teacher presents a new situation to which students can transfer their understanding of the skill. • Pairs evaluate an example of a statement and whether or not it is transferable to a new situation.

Consider the example below on persuasive writing focused specifically on the skill of finding relevant evidence to support claims, an essential skill that requires quite a bit of development.

1. **Opening:** The teacher opens the lesson with the objective of increasing our ability to find and use relevant *evidence* to support our claims in persuasive

writing. First, as a review from a previous lesson, he asks students to discuss the word *relevant* in small groups. Next, he asks students to share with a partner how this goal is connected to their previous learning on crafting claims.

2. **Minilesson:** The teacher conducts a think-aloud to show how he finds relevant evidence to support his claim that *the cafeteria should not serve fried foods.* The students share the steps he used with a partner in their own words.

3. **Work time:** Using a scaffolding technique, the teacher provides a claim along with several statements that could be used as evidence. Students work in pairs to identify which statements are good examples of relevant evidence and which ones are not. Following this step, students move to selecting evidence for their own claims using classroom resources the teacher has collected in advance. The teacher circulates and assists students who may need a bit more practice with another scaffolding technique.

4. **Generalize and debrief:** Students write statements about the role of relevant evidence in persuasive writing.

5. **Transfer:** At the start of the next lesson, the teacher presents a new claim and asks students to select relevant evidence from a list of statements to deepen students' understanding and practice.

Lesson Framework #4: Project-Based Learning

Learning centered around projects often provides meaning for students and is one way to make learning more organized and authentic and less fragmented from day to day. Many schools are adopting this method of instruction as a means to motivate students and make learning more relevant and inclusive. It is completely compatible with Concept-Based Curriculum and Instruction—we just need to be very careful to articulate conceptual goals from the start and keep them as the focus throughout.

We turn to the Buck Institute's Gold Standard Project-Based Learning to craft this lesson framework and provide guidance on how to blend these two important educational endeavors. The Buck Institute provides a clear definition of Project-Based Learning:

> Project Based Learning is a teaching method in which students gain knowledge and skills by working for an extended period of time to investigate and respond to an engaging and complex question, problem, or challenge. (What is Project-Based Learning? n.d.).

They also provide clear design elements, which are aligned to Concept-Based elements in the following ways:

1. Projects begin with clear knowledge, understanding, and skills.

2. Projects use an inquiry or inductive process to guide students toward discovery of understanding.

3. Projects start with and maintain a question or challenge, rather than a statement, to engage students and turn on the brain.

Consider each element of Gold Standard Project-Based Learning in Figure 4.5, as well as the slight modifications we make in applying this approach to Concept-Based units.

FIGURE 4.5   COMBINING PROJECT-BASED LEARNING WITH CONCEPT-BASED LEARNING

Gold Standard PBL Element	Traditional PBL	Concept-Based PBL Modifications
Key Knowledge, Understanding, and Success Skills	The project is focused on student learning goals, including standards-based content and skills such as critical thinking/problem solving, collaboration, and self-management.	The project is focused on conceptual learning goals, in addition to standards-based content and skills such as critical thinking/problem solving, collaboration, and self-management.
Challenging Problem or Question	The project is framed by a meaningful problem to solve or a question to answer, at the appropriate level of challenge.	The project is framed by a conceptual question or meaningful problem to be solved using conceptual understanding.
Sustained Inquiry	Students engage in a rigorous, extended process of asking questions, finding resources, and applying information.	Students inquire into several different contexts to inform conceptual understanding and apply it to solving the challenge, problem, or question.
Authenticity	The project features real-world context, tasks, and tools, quality standards, or impact—or speaks to students' personal concerns, interests, and issues in their lives.	Authenticity involves transfer of conceptual understanding to a real-world context.
Student Voice and Choice	Students make some decisions about the project, including how they work and what they create.	Students can make choices about the different contexts they investigate and may arrive at their own unique conceptual understandings. Theses choices are in addition to other choices in the project.

(Continued)

FIGURE 4.5 (Continued)

Gold Standard PBL Element	Traditional PBL	Concept-Based PBL Modifications
Reflection	Students and teachers reflect on learning, the effectiveness of their inquiry and project activities, the quality of student work, and obstacles and how to overcome them.	Students also reflect on the evolution of their conceptual understanding and effectiveness of transferring this understanding to a new situation.
Critique and Revision	Students give, receive, and use feedback to improve their process and products.	Student critique and revision includes a critique and revision of conceptual understanding and effectiveness of transfer.
Public Product	Students make their project work public by explaining, displaying, and/ or presenting it to people beyond the classroom.	Concepts and conceptual relationships are made explicit in the public product.

SOURCE: (first two columns) What Is Project-Based Learning? (n.d.).

It is important to realize that project-based learning does not happen in a single, stand-alone lesson. Therefore, a framework for planning Concept-Based projects should be used to design an entire unit of study, not just a lesson or two. There is just no way to build knowledge through sustained inquiry, or to critique and revise processes and products, in a few days. We suggest using this model for a three- to four-week project, minimum; often these projects last much longer.

When planning a Concept-Based project, we find it useful to create a student-facing document that outlines the project, establishes some criteria for success, and identifies major deadlines. Create a one-page letter to students that frames the challenge of the project. We love to use a modified version of the GRASPS (goal, role, audience, situation, public product, standards) model created by Wiggins and McTighe (2005) as a guideline, adding "concepts" to keep us focused on our conceptual goals:

- **Concepts:** Name the concepts that students will be investigating in this project.
- **Goal:** State a clear goal, so students know what they need to do with their understanding of the concepts.
- **Role:** Assign students a real-world role or perspective.
- **Audience:** Describe the real-world audience students should keep in mind when designing their final product
- **Situation:** Situate the question or problem in a specific context and describe it briefly.
- **Public product or performance:** Tell students what they are expected to create (an essay, skit, website, documentary, business proposal, etc.).

- **Standards for success:** Communicate the criteria for successful completion of the project. Consider including a rubric to measure the quality of the final product as well as checklists that outline the essential components you expect to be included.

Here's an example from a third-grade classroom. Note that while the acronym C-GRASPS helps educators remember the essential elements for framing a project, this is not necessarily the most natural order for explaining the elements to students. See if you can identify each element in the project below:

> How many times a day do we throw something away? Where does it all go? As the population of the earth increases, more and more trash is entering our environment. On average, Americans throw out over four pounds of garbage every day. Trash often ends up in our soil, air, and water, which can be a threat to our health. We will research three different kinds of waste: food waste, recyclable waste, and regular waste. We will look for patterns in each of these situations and come up with solutions for how we can reduce our impact on the environment at home and at school. We will present our proposals at the parent–teacher association meeting, urging them to help us take action on this important issue.

Teachers may choose to include the grading rubric alongside the document framing the C-GRASPS of the task. Alternately, it is sometimes beneficial to include students in the process of determining criteria for success. In the example above, for instance, the teacher may ask students to watch a video of a speaker proposing a solution at a public forum to analyze what good presentations include.

Once you have a vision for the project, consider the instructional principles and steps in Figure 4.6 as you plan for instruction.

Project-based learning is a powerful way for students to uncover conceptual relationships, because it puts their conceptual understanding to real-world use. To maximize the impact of your project, be sure to avoid these common pitfalls:

- It's easy to plan a project that is real-world, interesting, or hands-on without requiring deep investigation or transfer of the concepts. If you are new to this, it might help to start with the concepts and contexts you would normally teach in a unit, rather than starting with the real-world scenario that requires transfer of conceptual understanding. Just be sure to include conceptual understanding and evidence as categories in your rubric or scoring scheme.

- Too much student independence can lead to misunderstandings, as students tend to rush through the investigatory phase of the project in order to focus more on the product. Set up checkpoints or benchmarks to help guide the pace of each group's work and to formally assess student understanding as they move along.

FIGURE 4.6 PROJECT-BASED LESSON FRAMEWORK

Lesson Principle	Questions to Ask Yourself	Might Look Like
1. Hook students by introducing them to the conceptual question to be answered or problem to be solved (sometimes called a "launch").	• What conceptual relationships do I want students to uncover in this project? • How can I make this question or problem relevant, urgent, and interesting? • How can I get kids to wonder about the question or problem without feeding it to them? • How can I connect the concepts to students' emotions, personal interests and concerns, culture, or identity to draw them in?	• A gallery walk of photos, statistics, and quotes related to the problem to be solved (e.g., migrant crisis in Europe, global water shortages). • Watch a short video or read a short story through which the question might surface (e.g., read an e. e. cummings's poem and ponder the role of punctuation, grammar, and word order in writing). • Discuss a real-life or school-based scenario that correlates to the concepts (e.g., discussing a mother appeasing a toddler throwing a tantrum in a candy store before inquiring into the foreign policy of appeasing Hitler in the 1930s). • Partner with a local organization to extend a challenge or pose a question to students (e.g., a representative from a local watershed protection society comes to class to enlist student help in reducing pollution in local waterways). • Distribute a written overview of the project to students, complete with rubric and deadlines, to help them envision the challenge.
2. Help students plan their inquiry and build background knowledge.	• How much support and direction will I provide to students during the inquiry process? • Which contexts should all students study? Which other contexts might students choose to investigate as part of their inquiry?	• Students brainstorm possible approaches to the question or problem as a whole class while the teacher writes on the board. • Provide a sample research calendar to each group, and ask them to modify it or divide tasks among them.

TOOLS FOR TEACHING CONCEPTUAL UNDERSTANDING, ELEMENTARY

Lesson Principle	Questions to Ask Yourself	Might Look Like
	• What resources would best help students deeply inquire into the question or problem?	• Supply a list of resources for each context (books, videos, articles, images, etc.) to get students started. • Help students brainstorm ways to extend their inquiry: interviewing experts, taking a field trip, designing an experiment, conducting an opinion poll, et cetera. • Give students a written research guide that outlines your expectations (specific contexts they must study, optional contexts, types of acceptable sources).
3. Monitor student inquiry process and guide student reflection	• What scaffolding will students need to help them conduct their own research? • How will I serve as a coach for each group during the inquiry process? • What questions will I pose to students to challenge them? • How will I make sure students are focused on the concepts? • When and how will students reflect on their understanding and the inquiry process?	• Provide graphic organizers to help students organize information. • Ask students to keep a journal of their research (they should summarize their findings and also reflect on the inquiry process); provide comments and feedback. • "Interview" each group about the concepts at various intervals throughout the inquiry process.
4. Support students as they construct high-quality products through critique and revision.	• How will students know what quality work looks like? • How can I ensure that students thoughtfully critique their own and each other's work? • How will students know how to revise or strengthen weak areas of their product?	• Provide rubrics, checklists, and models of exemplary work. • Ask students to use formal critique and feedback protocols when responding to each other's work. • Bring in experts to provide feedback based on the standards of quality in your field.

(Continued)

FIGURE 4.6 (Continued)

Lesson Principle	Questions to Ask Yourself	Might Look Like
5. Organize students to publish or present their products to a real-world audience.	• Who is the primary audience for this work? How can I help students get the attention of their target audience? • Can we present these products off campus or outside of school hours? • How will students prepare to discuss their work with others?	• Invite the school community—parents, teachers, other students— to a "gallery opening" or "invention fair" with student products on display. • Conduct a "teach-in," where students present their conclusions to others in order to inform or persuade. • Organize a panel of experts—lawyers, engineers, environmentalists, college professors—to respond to and evaluate student speeches. • Post student videos to a YouTube channel, or create a website to convey student findings to the outside world.
6. Provide opportunities for reflection about the content and the process.	• How will students reflect on the conceptual relationships they uncovered, the facts that support these relationships, and the significance of their new understanding? • How will students reflect on their learning process? • How will students reflect on their role within the group and the group dynamic? • How will students reflect on the quality of their final product?	• Ask students to write journal entries using the prompt "At the start of the project I thought . . . , but then . . . , so now I think. . . ." • Have students record video blogs where they verbally express their reflections (similar to a reality show "confessional"). • Require students to write letters to their group-mates, the audience of their product, or you (the teacher) to explain how these people contributed to their learning. • Have groups write a group reflection in the form of advice for next year's students. • Have students list lessons learned on sticky notes and then categorize and debrief them as a class.

- Too little student independence defeats the purpose of the project-based model. Students need time and space to make mistakes and then to learn from them as they refine their understanding and product through feedback. When you notice students making mistakes, resist the urge to tell students what to do or think. Instead, ask questions and provide feedback that allows students to figure out how to improve on their own.

- Remember that the project-based model is a way of designing an entire unit of study, meaning that students must learn the required content and develop conceptual understanding *through* the project. Assigning a project at the end of a unit, after the required learning has already taken place, is not project-based learning, but rather an assessment of learning otherwise achieved. Both are valid classroom tools, but the structure here is meant to support project-based learning, not project-based assessment.

Lesson Framework #5: Personalized Learning

We are encouraged by the trend of learning adapted to the pace, needs, goals, interests and motivations of students rather than students constantly adapting to the average-oriented, one-size-fits-all instruction. We've included this lesson framework because personalized learning is a valuable method of teaching and learning. It is a relatively new and trendy phenomenon; therefore, we will take a moment to frame what it means to us.

First, what is personalized learning? Many people think of it as "learning at your own pace." We think this is an overly simplistic view. We prefer to think of it as each student *making meaning* for himself or herself, which is aligned to the philosophy of inductive or constructivist teaching. In this mode of thinking, it becomes clear that simply checking off tasks on a playlist that feels more like a "to do" list, without a demonstration of deep understanding, is not exactly revolutionary or great learning—even if you can check off those boxes in a different order or at a different rate than the student next to you.

Personalized learning is often presented as synonymous with technology. We value the role of technology in helping our young people learn better and faster—but personalized learning does not have to be dependent upon technology. We've added alternatives to learning exclusively from a laptop or tablet in this lesson framework.

Another, related tension with personalized learning lies in the importance of learning in a social context. Humans are social animals, and there is a lot of research to support students discussing ideas and learning from each other—which is hard to do if your path involves a lot of individual time with a screen. Also worth noting is that, at the time of this writing, very little technology can provide valuable feedback on the *quality* of student work. Tech can tell us "yes, you got it right" or "no, you didn't," but we know that deeper learning requires more than that. Therefore, we caution zealous implementers of personalized learning to be sure to include lots of human expert feedback on student work as well as time for kids to work together to construct meaning.

What troubles us the most, however, is that missing from the hype of truly transforming teaching and learning is that the *goals* often remain surface level. This is why we assert that a curriculum must go beyond the topic level before we even begin to talk about personalizing instruction. There is sometimes a corresponding component of eschewing standardization and adding new goals such as critical thinking and creativity. It is crucial to remember that *innovation requires expertise and a fundamental understanding of at least one discipline.* So let's not throw the baby out with the bathwater! That's the value of Concept-Based Curriculum.

Personalization often offers students more voice and choice in their learning. Concept-Based Curriculum naturally allows for more personalization particularly in the contexts that students explore in order to arrive at the conceptual relationships. Compare the two attempts at deeper learning for an English language arts class (Figure 4.7). Why does the Concept-Based unit naturally allow for more student choice?

FIGURE 4.7   TOPIC-BASED VERSUS CONCEPT-BASED UNIT

Topic-Based Unit	Concept-Based Unit
Students will analyze the character development and universal themes of *La Mariposa* by Francisco Jiménez.	Students will uncover and transfer the understanding that authors develop complexity of characters through dialogue, plot, and descriptive text. Conceptual Question: How do authors develop complexity of characters?

Through conceptual questions, the students are able to choose texts to read to arrive at their own conclusions. Students could be reading entirely different books, but with a focused goal of conceptual relationship, the teacher could facilitate rich discussions using the conceptual questions.

A diverse group funded by the Gates Foundation gathered to define personalized learning. *Personalized Learning: A Working Definition* (2014) published by *Education Week* outlines four key areas:

1. Learner profiles: Each student has an up-to-date record of his or her individual strengths, needs, motivations, and goals.

2. Personal learning paths: All students are held to clear, high expectations, but each student follows a customized path that responds and adapts based on the student's individual learning progress, motivations, and goals.

3. Competency-based progression: Each student's progress toward clearly defined goals is continually assessed. Students advance and earn credit as soon as they individually demonstrate mastery.

4. Flexible learning environments: Student needs drive the design of the learning environment. All operational elements—staffing plans, space utilization, and time allocation—respond and adapt to support students in achieving their goals.

A really important characteristic of personalized learning is *learning pathways*. The idea is to disassemble the learning hierarchy of certain lessons before others, place them all in front of students at the same time, and allow the students to learn not only at their own pace but in their own order. In the context of conceptual teaching and learning, we can plan different ways for students to collect information that will help them to answer the conceptual questions. Figure 4.8 contains a lesson framework for personalized learning with planning questions and suggestions for what each step might look like.

FIGURE 4.8   PERSONALIZED LEARNING LESSON FRAMEWORK

Lesson Principle	Questions to Ask Yourself	Might Look Like
1. Start with **conceptual questions** that target the statement of conceptual relationships of the unit.	• What conceptual relationships are at the heart of this unit? • How can I create conceptual questions that engage students and allow for deep thought right away? • What questions will allow me to gauge students' preinstructional understanding of the concepts?	• Students record initial thoughts about conceptual relationships in journal. • Groups draw nonlinguistic representations of the concept on chart paper and gallery walk to see breadth of class's thinking. • Small groups discuss conceptual questions, and teacher observes. • Teacher provides variety of sample relationship statements or images, and students explain which one aligns with their thinking and why.
2. Collect data for **learner profile**.	• What choices might I offer students that cater to their interests, strengths, motivations, and needs? • How can I use their personal goals in planning the instructional portion of this unit? • How can I involve students in the planning of the instructional portion of this unit?	• Students rank a list of possible contexts that target the conceptual relationships. • Teacher provides a list of skills associated with the unit, and students sort them based on which are current strengths and which need improvement. • Students rank interest in different potential activities for the learner pathways.

(Continued)

FIGURE 4.8 (Continued)

Lesson Principle	Questions to Ask Yourself	Might Look Like
3. Brainstorm different potential **learner paths**.	• What choices might I offer students that cater to their interests, strengths, motivations, and needs? • What resources already exist that help build background knowledge and understanding for this unit? • What do I need to create in order to build background knowledge or understanding? • How can I be creative in providing unique and varied experiences that will help students uncover the conceptual relationships? • How can I train people or edit resources in order to build conceptual understanding?	• Teacher creates a playlist for the unit, and students move at their own pace in order to uncover the conceptual relationship. • Students choose between one-on-one tutoring, online learning, and small-group instruction that will help them uncover the conceptual relationship. • Students interview different experts about the conceptual relationship of the unit. • Students conduct their own research in order to uncover the conceptual relationships of the unit.
4. Determine how students will demonstrate **mastery** and **progress**.	• How can students frequently measure their progress? • How can students use the data on the formative assessments in order to set goals and move at their own pace? • What different modalities (essay, video, etc.) can students use to demonstrate progress and mastery? • What is acceptable for mastery of this unit, and what will early completers do once they demonstrate mastery?	• Teacher creates formative assessments in advance and allows students to complete them frequently. • Teacher creates a rubric that allows for multiple modes of performance (video, essay, 3D design). • Students use formative assessments to determine their pace. • Students choose one of several novel situations as a context in which to explain their understanding. • Early completers design their own project for deepening their understanding or increasing capacity from their needs list.

Lesson Principle	Questions to Ask Yourself	Might Look Like
5. Determine how students will **transfer** understanding to a new, complex situation.	• How will students test out their statements of conceptual relationships in new contexts?	• Students pair up to test their statements in each other's contexts. • Students choose different contexts to test their relationship. • Peers evaluate each other's relationships. • Mentors provide new contexts to test out the relationships. • Pairs brainstorm situations in which they could use their new idea (transferability).
6. Think creatively about the **learning environment** and allocation of **resources.**	• What staffing roles will maximize student choice and variance in pacing for this unit? • How can I efficiently use time to allow students to pursue their own interests and goals for this unit? • How can we build connection with other students and adults in this unit? • What community resources are available?	• Tutors provide one-on-one or small-group instruction • A variety of experts come to school, and students rotate through different stations to collect evidence to address the conceptual questions. • Students visit the local library to collect evidence to address the conceptual questions. • Parents donate supplies to allow hands-on discovery of the conceptual relationships.
7. Determine ways to **evaluate** and **adapt** to learner needs.	• How often will I solicit student feedback on the status of the unit? • How can I adapt learner pathways, resources, and the environment to meet the needs of the students?	• Teachers meet weekly to discuss each student's progress and brainstorm ways to adapt learner pathways. • Students meet weekly with teacher one-on-one to discuss their progress and brainstorm ways to adapt learner pathways.

These five lesson frameworks demonstrate ways in which we can ensure different instructional models can be aligned to Concept-Based Curriculum design. As long as conceptual understanding is the goal, and students use a fact base from a specific context to uncover the conceptual relationship, you are on the right track as a conceptual teacher. The more practice students have at transferring their understanding to new situations, the deeper their learning.

Conclusion

This chapter provides five instructional frameworks to help guide you as you experiment with lesson planning for deep, conceptual learning. This is not an exhaustive list of how you can foster students' ability to uncover conceptual relationships and transfer their understanding. No matter what instructional design method you use or your school uses, remember to keep conceptual relationships as the goal as you plan, and you will be well on your way.

Chapter Review

- How do conceptual questions help students learn? How do thought-provoking questions help teachers plan?
- How do specific contexts deepen student understanding about conceptual relationships?
- Why is it essential for students to use factual evidence to support their statements of conceptual relationships?
- How might you convince someone that teaching conceptually is worth the time it takes?

CHAPTER 5

How Do We Design Assessments for Conceptual Understanding?

Having worked in schools across the world and education spectrum, we know that assessment is a tricky and loaded topic—the spark of countless heated debates. (We've been in many!) Each of you reading this book lives in a different ecosystem of evaluating student progress. For some of you, the state test might be the be-all-end-all of your school's vision of assessment. Others might be pushing your colleagues to experiment with dialogical assessment, abandon traditional grades, and focus on student reflection. Our hope is that this chapter will support you in making meaning of and measuring student progress toward worthwhile goals in an authentic way, regardless of where you find yourselves on that spectrum.

In the Concept-Based classroom, the primary purpose of assessment is to provide feedback on the learning process to improve student learning. The word *assessment* comes from the Latin verb *assidere* meaning "to sit with," implying it is something we do *with* and *for* students and not *to* students (Green, 1998). Assessing young students should help us understand where they are and how we can help them grow, as well as facilitate students' understanding of their own growth.

We dream of a teaching and learning setting where students are internally motivated to learn, move at a pace that is appropriately challenging, and receive something more like scout badges for demonstration of skills, rather than numerical scores. We also believe that conceptual understanding is something that doesn't fit into the paradigm of checking objectives off a list as they are mastered. Conceptual understandings should *continuously be refined and deepened* as students grow, so assessment for conceptual understanding should facilitate the improvement of thought.

Four Principles for Assessment in a Concept-Based Classroom

1. **Transfer is the ultimate goal.** As conceptual learning guru Lois Lanning (2009) writes, "The most important skills, knowledge, attitudes, and understandings that students acquire through schools are relevant because they have value and application in later times and in different circumstances" (p. 13). We ultimately want students to use their conceptual understanding to understand and transform the world. That means these understandings cannot be inert knowledge, but rather keys to unlocking new situations. If that is our goal, our assessments need to provide insight on students' progress toward transferring their understanding to new situations.

2. **Mistakes are important.** In the Concept-Based classroom, stumbles and missteps are expected, valued, and made meaningful. We must provide opportunities for students to *safely* test out their initial understandings, notice what needs improvement, and continue working until they reach a satisfactory level.

3. **It's not about right or wrong—it's about progress and evidence.** Students are often trained to look for the right answer. With assessment for conceptual understanding, we need to shift their questions from "Is this right?" to "Does this evidence/example support my understanding?" and "How can I deepen my understanding of these ideas?" Learning best happens in a culture of *continuous growth* where students can track their own progress, seeing their efforts transform simplistic understandings into profound, sophisticated ones.

4. **Feedback throughout—not just at the end.** Students need constructive feedback that they can use to improve throughout their exploration of a concept. Rather than waiting until the end of a unit to receive feedback or scores, students should be in constant conversation with teachers and peers about how they can deepen their understanding.

5. In practice, these principles translate into a classroom where teachers constantly collect nonpunitive evidence of student understanding. Students collect evidence of and set their own goals for improving their level of understanding. Students also receive feedback that helps them figure out what to do next.

> Concept-Based teachers plan for both summative and ongoing formative assessment upfront.

This means that Concept-Based teachers plan for both summative and ongoing formative assessment upfront. Imagine you are teaching a unit where students explore the relationship between human

FIGURE 5.1   ASSESSMENT OVERVIEW

When?	Assessment Step	Examples
At the beginning of the unit	Preassess understanding of *individual concepts.*	*Define habitat in your own words.* *Define human needs in your own words.* Provide feedback on any misconceptions or shallow understandings.
After a few lessons	Measure *initial* understanding of conceptual *relationships.*	*What is the relationship between human needs and habitats? Use evidence to support your answer.*
Throughout the unit	Measure *deepening and refining* of understanding of conceptual relationships.	Repeat the question above, asking students to incorporate additional examples from your exploration in class and use a rubric to evaluate their progress. Also ask them to think of ways to improve.
At least once before the summative assessment; usually toward the end of the unit	Measure ability to *transfer* understanding of conceptual relationships.	Provide students with several inputs (articles, examples, experiments, etc.) about a new situation, and ask them to make predictions, solve a problem, or explain phenomena in terms of the concepts. Then ask them to reflect on the process of transferring their understanding to a new situation. *Based on your understanding of the relationship between habitats and human needs,* *. . . what might happen next in this scenario?* *. . . why did X occur in this situation?* *. . . how could we resolve X problem?* *How did your understanding of habitats and human needs help you better understand this new situation? Did this situation clarify, contradict, or confirm your understanding of human needs and habitats? Give examples to support your answers.* Provide students with feedback on their ability to transfer their understanding using the rubric and engage in dialogue with students about the process of transfer.
End of unit (summative assessment)	Measure *transfer* and *depth* of understanding of conceptual relationships.	Provide students with several inputs (articles, examples, experiments, etc.) about a new situation, and ask them to make predictions, solve a problem, or explain phenomena in terms of the concepts. Rate student performances using a rubric. See questions above.

(Continued)

FIGURE 5.1 (Continued)

When?	Assessment Step	Examples
End of unit (reflection)	Measure metacognitive awareness of understanding and growth.	Ask students to assess their own understanding using a rubric. *Write a reflection about where your understanding falls on the rubric, defend why it falls there with evidence from your work, and explain how your thinking progressed throughout the unit.*

needs and habitats. You might create an assessment plan like the one shown in the overview in Figure 5.1.

Throughout the unit, the teacher is always gathering information about where students are and using that information to provide feedback and make adjustments. Figure 5.1 lays out a wholesale shift in assessment toward the Concept-Based approach. It is not necessary, however, as you begin to experiment with this type of assessment that you shift all your assessment to this model. Instead, start by trying out the principles discussed above in small ways, and see what works for your students in your context.

Designing Summative Tasks

Summative assessment, or assessment *of* learning, occurs at the *end point* in the learning journey, most often at the end of a unit. Whether this assessment takes the form of a test or oral presentation or written report, the purpose is to evaluate the extent to which a student has achieved the goals of a unit of study. Most often, summative assessments result in numerical scores or letter grades of some kind. This distinguishes summative assessment from formative assessment, or assessment *for* learning. Formative assessment generally results in feedback to help students improve.

We assert that summative assessment is—in terms of teaching and learning—far less important than formative assessment. Research (Brookhart, 2008) confirms that when there is a final grade on an assignment, students often focus on the letter or number and disregard the substantive comments. Who can blame them? If grades are "final" judgments of their work, there is no reason to expend energy thinking about improvement; the grade won't change.

This poses a challenge for the Concept-Based classroom: What role does summative assessment play when we're aiming for a culture of *continuous* growth and refinement of thought? If we view the development of conceptual understanding as an *ongoing* process, what is the value in end-point assessment?

Although formative feedback is the stuff that drives learning, it is the summative assessment that provides a clear picture of the learning goal in mind. A well-designed summative assessment answers the question, Where do we want to end up? In this way, summative tasks are essential to the Concept-Based classroom. Envisioning an end point can help motivate students—*by the end of this unit I'll be able to do that!*—and help teachers target their feedback and advice to ensure student success. Since the goal is transfer, summative assessments should be designed around interesting, real-world scenarios that demand the transfer of conceptual understanding.

> Summative assessments should be designed around interesting, real-world scenarios that demand the transfer of conceptual understanding.

It is easy to mistakenly assess and evaluate students' ability to recall facts learned in class rather than ask students to generate their own understanding of the relationship between concepts, or to transfer that understanding to a new situation. In Chapter 1, we discussed Anderson and Krathwohl's (2001) revision of Bloom's taxonomy and the addition of the knowledge dimension. For a moment, though, we'll return to the cognitive processes: remember, understand, apply, analyze, evaluate, and create (see Figure 5.2).

FIGURE 5.2 A TAXONOMY FOR LEARNING, TEACHING, AND ASSESSING

Knowledge Dimension	Cognitive Process Dimension					
	Remember	Understand	Apply	Analyze	Evaluate	Create
Factual Knowledge						
Conceptual Knowledge						
Procedural Knowledge						
Metacognitive Knowledge						

SOURCE: Anderson/Krathwohl/Airasian/Cruikshank/Mayer/Pintrich/Raths/Wittrock, *A Taxonomy for Learning, Teaching, and Assessing: A Revision of Bloom's Taxonomy of Educational Objectives*, Abridged Edition, 1st Ed., ©2001. Reprinted by permission of Pearson Education, Inc., New York, New York.

When we are assessing conceptual understanding, we need to avoid mistaking students' ability to remember facts for their having a deep and complex understanding of conceptual relationships. For example, if we ask students to discuss what they have learned within a context they are already familiar with, often they can easily regurgitate what we have covered in class. It's sometimes tempting to go through this process and hear students parrot back to us our own thinking. If we do this, however, we are not actually assessing students' understanding, just their ability to recall information they have already learned.

In order to truly assess students' understanding, or any other higher thinking process, it is critical that we ask them to transfer their understanding to a novel situation. Consider the example in Figure 5.3. to see how students might transfer their understanding to a new situation.

As stated in Chapter 1, Perkins and Salomon (1988) refer to this as "high-road transfer," meaning it is not simply applying the same rote procedure in a new situation.

FIGURE 5.3   EXAMPLE OF TRANSFER OF UNDERSTANDING

Imagine fourth- or fifth-grade students exploring the relationship between migration and environmental challenges. If in class we discussed this conceptual relationship in the context of 19th century settlement in the New World, for the assessment we might ask students to show their understanding of this same relationship in the context of modern migration and the Syrian migration situation. Initially, this way of assessing might feel uncomfortable to both us and our students. We've heard teachers and students say "But we didn't learn this."

Our answer is "Yes, you didn't learn it, but you can figure it out!" The goal is for students to apply and stretch their understanding with a new factual context. In this example, we will avoid mistaking students' ability to remember facts about the topic of pioneers for true understanding. Instead we'll be able to assess how well students are able to *transfer* their understanding of modern challenges and the migration to a new situation. The ideas are the same, but the facts are different. Providing different facts allows student thinking about the conceptual relationship to become visible.

Instead, we are asking students to build their understanding, abstract the relationship between concepts, and apply that understanding to a new factual situation. Students use their conceptual understanding as a lens to interpret the new situation, and that situation in turn refines their lens. Figure 5.4 illustrates various methods for different types of transfer. Notice the bottom right box where students apply new knowledge to *dissimilar situations.*

This same principle is evident in assessment expert Susan Brookhart's (2010) guidelines for assessing higher–order thinking. Brookhart advises assessment designers

FIGURE 5.4   VISIBLE LEARNING FOR LITERACY

Hugging to Promote Low-Road Transfer *Students are learning to apply skills and knowledge.*	Bridging to Promote High-Road Transfer *Students are learning to make links across concepts.*
The teacher is associating prior knowledge with new knowledge.	Students are using analogies and metaphors to illustrate connections across disciplines or content.
Students are categorizing information.	Students are deriving rules and principles based on examples.
The teacher is modeling and thinking aloud.	Students are thinking metacognitively and reflectively to plan and organize.
Students are summarizing and rehearsing knowledge.	Students are creating new and original content.
The teacher creates role-play and simulation opportunities for students to apply new knowledge to parallel situations.	Students are applying new knowledge to dissimilar situations.

SOURCE: Fisher, Frey, & Hattie (2016, p. 110).

to use novel material and to present something for students to think about. Again these guidelines help us—as assessment designers—to narrow in on what we actually hope to evaluate: students thinking about conceptual relationships. If we don't give students something to think about (text, a video, an image) we are expecting them to draw from their memory, and therefore assessing at least partially their ability to recall information. Similarly, if the material we provide isn't novel, students can rely on their memories rather than having to apply their conceptual understanding. In order to truly assess students' conceptual understanding, we need to ask them to apply that understanding to situations they have not yet seen.

> In order to truly assess students' conceptual understanding, we need to ask them to apply that understanding to situations they have not yet seen.

Erickson and Lanning (2014) advise us to select one or two of the most important conceptual relationships of the unit, along with the corresponding knowledge and skills, as the first step in designing the assessment. The next step is figuring out an engaging scenario that will capture the hearts and minds of students. Figure 5.5 shows Erickson's Concept-Based assessment formula with an example.

FIGURE 5.5   ERICKSON'S CONCEPT-BASED ASSESSMENT FORMULA

What (the unit focus): Government

Why (the generalization): Humans develop different systems to organize and structure societies.

How (the engaging scenario for students): Throughout this unit, you have been increasing your expertise about the different ways we can structure a democracy. We have talked about majority rule and minority protection. California is a state that puts a lot of issues to direct vote to the whole population. Many other states allow their legislature to vote on most issues. Our current governor is trying to decide whether or not to put a controversial issue on the ballot for everyone to cast a vote. Which do you think is the better way to organize and structure society? You will take a stand and then write a persuasive letter to the editor on the issue.

For helping to plan the engaging scenario, we like Wiggins and McTighe's (2005) acronym: GRASPS (goal, role, audience, situation, public product, standards). Figure 5.6 contains a few prompts adapted from their model that is designed to help stimulate thinking about an engaging scenario.

It is fairly easy to assess students' abilities to remember factual information. Designing ways to measure understanding, application, analysis, evaluation, and synthesis, however, can be quite difficult. Brookhart (2010) provides sage advice on how to achieve this goal, and a few key ideas are included in Figure 5.7.

Over the years, we've experimented with different ways to clearly measure higher-order thinking. The most important step is to isolate exactly what it is we want to

FIGURE 5.6   WIGGINS AND MCTIGHE'S PERFORMANCE TASK DESIGN PROMPTS

Goal: Demonstrate your understanding of the relationship between . . . and . . . (concepts).

Role:

You are. . . .

You have been asked to. . . .

Your job is. . . .

Audience:

Your clients are. . . .

The target audience is. . . .

You need to convince. . . .

Situation:

The context you find yourself in is. . . .

The challenge involves dealing with. . . .

Product, Performance, and Purpose:

You will create a . . . in order to. . . .

You need to develop . . . so that. . . .

Standards and Criteria for Success:

Your performance needs to. . . .

Your work will be judged by. . . .

Your product must meet the following standards. . . .

SOURCE: Wiggins and McTighe, 2005.

FIGURE 5.7   BROOKHART'S PRINCIPLES FOR ASSESSING HIGHER-ORDER THINKING

Assessing higher-order thinking almost always involves three additional principles:

- Present something for students to think *about,* usually in the form of introductory text, visuals, scenarios, resource material, or problems of some sort.

- Use novel material—material that is new to the student, not covered in class and thus subject to recall.

- Distinguish between level of difficulty (easy versus hard) and level of thinking (lower-order thinking or recall versus higher-order thinking), and control for each separately.

measure. We have found that too often there is a lot of "noise" crowding out the exact element we are trying to measure. What we do now is measure factual recall through ongoing assessment. But on the summative assessment, we try to provide new factual information and scaffold the assessment as much as possible so that we are better able to see students' deeper thinking about the conceptual relationships. Figure 5.8 provides some ideas for scaffolding to higher-ordered thinking.

FIGURE 5.8   SCAFFOLDING STRATEGIES FOR ASSESSING HIGHER-ORDERED THINKING

Provide a word bank, formula, or other factual information.

Provide a list of steps for a procedure.

Edit texts to make them shorter or more age appropriate.

Provide scaffolding questions that call attention to important points.

Break the assessment into parts.

Review the novel situation together in class to ensure comprehension.

Make the presentation visually pleasing.

Provide images, maps, and/or videos to provide background knowledge of novel situation.

Streamline it; take out any parts that are not necessary.

Make the directions crystal clear.

To take the task design one step further, we frequently ask students to take action based on their unit of study. This is aligned with the mission and goals of the International Baccalaureate curriculum along with the mission and values of many schools that want students to take responsibility and become engaged in the community. It provides relevance and meaning and can be incredibly motivating. Throughout the unit, we carefully move from academic, low-road transfer of learning to more complex, high-road, real-world transfer of learning (see Figure 5.9). The ultimate goal is that the summative assessments of each unit measure students' ability to transfer what they've learned to a novel, complex, real-world situation, usually a problem of some sort. And then we want them to do something about it!

FIGURE 5.9   WHERE INNOVATION HAPPENS

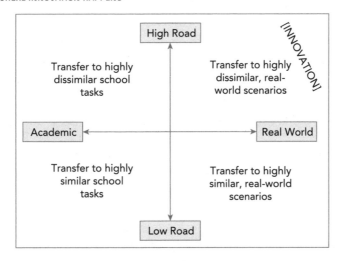

The Constitutional Rights Foundation along with the Close Up Foundation published *Active Citizenship Today Field Guide* (2nd edition, 2005). This guide is an extremely useful tool for guiding both teachers and students on specific, simple

techniques for taking action. Figure 5.10 contains a list of ways to take action that are explained in more detail in that text.

FIGURE 5.10   WAYS TO TAKE ACTION

Ways to Take Action
• Use social media for an awareness campaign.
• Volunteer with existing organizations.
• Write letters to officials.
• Start a letter-writing campaign.
• Start a petition.
• Speak in public.
• Make a leaflet.
• Write a newsletter.
• Raise awareness through art (mural, play, video).
• Host a debate.
• Conduct a sit-in.
• Conduct a teach-in.
• Write a letter to the editor.
• Create a press release for an event.
• Write a public service announcement.
• Lobby politicians.
• Host a fund-raiser.

Putting all of these elements together, we've created an adapted Concept-Based performance assessment tool, which can be used each time we design a summative task. Figures 5.11 and 5.12 provide two examples of its use; Figure 5.11 is from a first-grade health unit, and Figure 5.12 is from a fourth-grade unit on government.

Designing Formative Tasks

Formative assessment is only as good as the information it provides about where students are and where to go next. Keeping the goal of the summative assessment in mind, teachers can use formative assessments to check in on student progress throughout the unit, ensuring that they have the tools for success on the final task. In an elementary classroom, formative assessments are often mixed with daily lessons or learning. When teachers carefully observe students during the learning process, they can understand what the students know and help to plan the next steps of teaching.

Formative assessment is only as good as the information it provides about where students are and where to go next.

FIGURE 5.11 GRADE 1 EXAMPLE

J. Stern's Adapted Concept-Based Assessment Tool	
Step 1: The unit focus	Health
Step 2: The conceptual relationship	Meeting our physical and emotional needs helps to make us happy.
Step 3: The engaging, novel scenario, problem, or issue	Today we have some new friends in our classroom, little stuffed dolls. Each one of you will take the doll home and attend to his or her physical and emotional needs. After the weekend, you will explain to the class what you did at home with your new friend to ensure his or her happiness.
Step 4: Scaffolding strategies to assess higher-ordered thinking	As a class, we will review the difference between physical and emotional needs as well as identify the ones we have explored during the unit. Students will take a few minutes in class to select ones they think will be the most important to meet over the weekend to ensure the happiness of their new friend. We will also model the steps for a good presentation and refer to our pictorial list as a reminder right before the presentations.
Step 5: How students will take action	The class will vote on the following two options: Students can select the most important physical needs (e.g. food, clothing, soap) and then host a drive to collect and donate these goods to a local shelter OR students can select the most important emotional needs (e.g. kindness, safety) and try to implement that idea with a friend during recess.

While formative assessments are meant to help teachers plan for next steps in instruction, they are also meant to empower students to plan for next steps in learning. The report, *Growing Success: Assessment, Evaluation and Reporting in Ontario's Schools* (2010), makes an important point about the role of assessment in schools:

> Assessment plays a critical role in teaching and learning and should have as its goal the development of students as independent and autonomous learners. As an integral part of teaching and learning, assessment should be planned concurrently with instruction and integrated seamlessly into the learning cycle to inform instruction, guide next steps, and help teachers and students monitor students' progress towards achieving learning goals (p. 29).

Notice that one key goal of assessment is to help students gain independence and autonomy. This means that we need a formative assessment plan that deeply involves

FIGURE 5.12 GRADE 4 EXAMPLE

J. Stern's Adapted Concept-Based Assessment Tool	
Step 1: The unit focus	Government
Step 2: The conceptual relationship	Humans develop different systems to organize and structure societies.
Step 3: The engaging, novel scenario, problem, or issue	Throughout this unit, you have been increasing your expertise about the different ways we can structure a democracy. We have talked about majority rule and minority protection. California is a state that puts a lot of issues to direct vote to the whole population. Many other states allow their legislature to vote on most issues. Our current governor is trying to decide whether or not to put a controversial issue on the ballot for everyone to cast a vote. Which do you think is the better way to organize and structure society? Should the state legislature decide, or should the people vote on the issue directly? You will take a stand and then write a persuasive letter to the editor on the issue.
Step 4: Scaffolding strategies to assess higher-ordered thinking	We will review the novel situation in class to ensure comprehension. We will post a word bank and a list of steps for writing a persuasive essay on the board as they write, to remind them of the process and key terminology. Students will be allowed to use dictionaries, thesauruses, and spell-check as they write. Once they decide on which stance to take, they can work in groups to brainstorm their arguments and will peer-edit their letters before sending them.
Step 5: How students will take action	Write and submit a letter to the editor of a newspaper of their choice on this current issue.

students, making them our partners in developing learning goals, giving and receiving feedback, and monitoring progress.

> We need a formative assessment plan that deeply involves students, making them our partners in developing learning goals, giving and receiving feedback, and monitoring progress.

Think about it this way: Formative assessment is both assessment *for* learning and assessment *as* learning. During assessment *for* learning, teachers collect information to monitor student progress. This is where the teacher identifies students' needs, provides descriptive feedback, identifies next steps, and differentiates instruction. During assessment *as* learning, students collect information about their own learning. This includes identifying their own achievements and challenges and providing feedback to other students, as well as making adjustments in their approach to learning and reflecting on their progress.

Figure 5.13 summarizes the purposes of assessment, the nature of assessment, and the uses of assessment information (Growing Success, p. 31). When planning a

FIGURE 5.13   TYPES OF ASSESSMENT

Purpose of Classroom Assessment	Nature of Assessment	Use of Information
Assessment *for* learning "Assessment for learning is the process of seeking and interpreting evidence for use by learners and their teachers to decide where the learners are in their learning, where they need to go, and how best to get there." (Assessment for Learning, 2002, p. 2)	Diagnostic assessment occurs before instruction begins so teachers can determine students' readiness to learn new knowledge and skills, as well as obtain information about their interests and learning preferences.	The information gathered is used by teachers and students to determine what students already know and can do with respect to the knowledge and skills identified in the overall and specific expectations, so teachers can plan instruction and assessment that are differentiated and personalized and work with students to set appropriate learning goals.
	Formative assessment occurs frequently and in an ongoing manner during instruction, while students are still gaining knowledge and practicing skills.	The information gathered is used by teachers to monitor students' progress toward achieving the overall and specific expectations, so that teachers can provide timely and specific descriptive feedback to students, scaffold next steps, and differentiate instruction and assessment in response to student needs.
Assessment *as* learning "Assessment as learning focuses on the explicit fostering of students' capacity over time to be their own best assessors, but teachers need to start by presenting and modeling external, structured opportunities for students to assess themselves" (Western and Northern Canadian protocol, p. 42)	Formative assessment occurs frequently and in an ongoing manner during instruction, with support, modeling, and guidance from the teacher.	The information gathered is used by students to provide feedback to other students (peer assessment), monitor their own progress toward achieving their learning goals (self-assessment), make adjustments in their learning approaches, reflect on their learning, and set individual goals for learning.

(Continued)

FIGURE 5.13   (Continued)

Purpose of Classroom Assessment	Nature of Assessment	Use of Information
Assessment *of* learning "Assessment of learning is the assessment that becomes public and results in statements or symbols about how well students are learning. It often contributes to pivotal decisions that will affect students' futures. (Western and northern Canadian Protocol, p. 55)	Summative assessment occurs at or near the end of a period of learning, and may be used to inform further instruction.	The information gathered is used by the teacher to summarize learning at a given point of time. This summary is used to make judgments about the quality of student learning on the basis of established criteria, to assign a value to represent that quality, and to support the communication of information about achievement to students themselves, parents, teachers, and others.

SOURCE: © Queen's Printer for Ontario, 2010.

Concept-Based unit, it is important to plan for all three aspects of assessment: assessment *for* learning, assessment *as* learning, and assessment *of* learning.

In the Concept-Based classroom, formative assessment must do two things:

1. Make students' current thinking about the conceptual relationship visible
2. Leverage effective feedback to push student thinking forward

It is also important to look at the summative assessment and design formative tasks that give students opportunities to practice for the final task. We cannot expect students to know how to do an oral presentation without having practiced during formative assessments, where they receive feedback for improvement.

For example, consider a Grade 1 class working toward the following generalization:

> Communities have natural and built features and provide services that help meet the needs of the people who live and work there (adapted from The Ontario Curriculum, 2013).

The summative task might be this:

> In your **group,** design a community and create a 3-D model or a drawing to show what the community is like. Include at least two **natural features** and two **built features** in your community. Then you will **present** your work to the class and explain how your community functions, including how each feature responds to the needs of the people living in the community. Your teacher will assign you a **scenario** that will guide your presentation.

Notice what is in bold. Students should have ample experience with this knowledge and these concepts and skills prior to attempting the final task. Therefore, teachers must plan opportunities for students to work in groups, explore a variety of natural and built features present in real communities, and present to an audience.

An aligned formative task might take place during drama class:

> Students work in groups to create a tableau scene involving daily activities in their community—a walk in the park, a trip to the grocery store, a day at school. The teacher and other students can ask them questions about the community features—both built and natural—that play a role in the scene. The teacher might coach students in the moment: *Could you be more specific? What is an example to show what you mean? I'm having a tough time hearing you; let's try that again a little louder.* Students then reflect on their performance and give peer-to-peer feedback about working collaboratively with a group.

Notice that this formative task gives students a chance to explore ideas and practice skills in a fun, low-stakes way. Throughout the unit, the teacher should plan several such activities in order to gather information about where students are and use that information to provide feedback and make adjustments.

When students participate in formative assessment, they have opportunities to improve. The assessment is valuable because students are still working toward their final goal. In addition, formative assessment provides information to you as the teacher that helps you adjust instruction. For example, if you notice during formative assessment that many students have the same misunderstanding, you may choose to directly address that misunderstanding through a lesson or learning experience. In short, the goal of formative assessment is to provide opportunities for both students and teachers to reflect on progress and adjust, revise, or refine their work.

The Power of Effective Feedback

Teacher feedback on student work can be a powerful tool to dramatically improve student learning. However, the *quality* of the feedback is essential—low-quality feedback can actually have negative effects on student growth. Feedback cannot simply say, "You are not at the learning goal yet." It should indicate exactly where on the learning journey a student is, which habits or strategies the student is using that might be working or might need to be changed, and give the student ideas for what to do next. It must demonstrate a belief in students' capacity to reach the goal even while providing specific growth areas. To be effective, feedback must also be well timed to help push a student's thinking to the next level. As Brookhart (2008) explains in her book *How to Give Effective Feedback to Your Students,* "Feedback . . .

is just-in-time, just-for-me information delivered when and where it can do the most good" (p. 1).

Berger (2003) suggests that feedback—or critique as he refers to it—should be kind, helpful, and specific. These straightforward and simple guidelines help both teachers and students provide feedback to one another. Remember, the teacher does not need to be the only person providing feedback. Students can review one another's work and share ideas for improvement. In addition, students can reflect on their own work and revise for improvement.

At the elementary level, it is particularly important to model effective feedback and offer ample opportunities for students to practice giving feedback to each other. Sentence stems like those below can be a big help in guiding self-assessment and peer critique.

Ask students to explain and reflect upon their choices (using reflection sheets, sticky notes, or note cards):

- One aspect of my work that I'm proud of is. . . .
- I feel good about this piece because. . . .
- This is quality work because. . . .
- If I did this piece again, I would improve it by. . . .
- One thing I'd like to change about my work is. . . .
- I would like someone to help me . . . in order to make this better.

During peer assessment, students can use similar prompts to provide feedback and suggestions:

- One aspect of this work that I admire is. . . .
- One strength I see is. . . .
- This is quality work because. . . .
- One way to improve might be. . . .
- The part of this project that needs more work is. . . .

In the Concept-Based classroom, it is essential for teachers to give feedback on students' intellectual products—like statements of conceptual relationship—not just the physical products they make. It is nice for students to create neat, attractive work, but it is even more important that they show strong understanding of the concepts of a unit. Figure 5.14 contains a few examples of feedback and our commentary on what it communicates to the student.

Of course, feedback is only useful if students are supported in using the feedback to make specific improvements. Therefore, it is important for Concept-Based teachers to plan ample time for revision and reflection. Figure 5.15 shows a simple tool to help students think through feedback and put it to good use:

FIGURE 5.14 SAMPLE FEEDBACK AND COMMENTARY

Sample Feedback	Thoughts on the Feedback
The statement you wrote shows the relationship between two concepts. Your explanation and example support your statement about one concept. What other concept can you think of that relates to your example?	This feedback is focused on the goal of conceptual understanding and gives specific instructions on what is missing. It is also descriptive and not evaluative. It tries to be forward thinking and solution oriented without giving the answer.
You used a lot of examples to support your statement of conceptual relationship. That makes it a really compelling statement. How did you think of examples we had not talked about in class?	This feedback is positive and descriptive. It is likely for a student who may have been previously struggling with coming up with examples outside of class. The question allows the student to reflect on how she achieved this to help her continue on this path toward success.
Wow! This statement is complex and precise. The examples clearly support the relationship between the concepts in the statement. Nice work! How might you increase the sophistication of the conceptual relationship to take it to the next level?	This is descriptive, positive feedback for a student who is well on track for the learning target. It conveys enthusiasm for the student's work while also pushing him to keep thinking, promoting a culture of continuous growth.

FIGURE 5.15 PROCESSING FEEDBACK TOOL

The feedback I received was. . . .	So I decided to. . . .	Now my work is better because. . . .	Next time I will remember to. . . .

This framework also helps students prepare to discuss their work with the teacher and their peers.

Student Self-Assessment and Goal Setting

Self-assessment and goal setting take time to learn how to do well. In an elementary classroom, these skills often need to be modeled and explicitly taught by the teacher. Students must understand and internalize the criteria for successful performance in order to both set goals and evaluate their progress.

This is particularly important in the Concept-Based classroom. Students must learn to distinguish sophisticated, well-supported understandings of the conceptual relationships from superficial, poorly supported ones. This means that Concept-Based teachers must take the time to involve students in creating rubrics and evaluating sample statements of conceptual relationship.

Consider starting with a blank or partially filled-in rubric, like the one in Figure 5.16. Ask students to brainstorm what expert work might look like. As they come up with descriptors, push them to think of examples that illustrate what they mean, and record both on the board or a piece of chart paper for the class to see. Then ask them to think about work that is off track—incomplete, inaccurate, unclear, et cetera—and record these ideas as well.

Another approach would be to show students a few samples of excellent and poor work—either teacher-created work or samples saved from previous years—and ask them to explain what makes one product better than the other. This helps bring meaning to the criteria in the rubric and gives students a strong sense of the goal they are aiming for.

FIGURE 5.16   BLANK RUBRIC

	1–Off-track work	2	3	4–Expert work
Description:				
Example:				

Provide students with access to the rubric before, during, and after the assessment. Students can practice with the rubric, tuning their understanding of it through peer and teacher feedback. During the assessment, they may refer to the rubric to think about how they can improve their responses. After the assessment, students can reflect on their own work and self-assess.

Checklists can also help students to assess their own work. For instance, students might use the checklist in Figure 5.17 to determine the criteria their statements of conceptual relationship have met:

FIGURE 5.17   SELF-ASSESSMENT CHECKLIST

My statement . . .
- Includes the concepts.
- Tells how the concepts are related to each other.
- Is clear and accurate.
- Is supported by specific examples.
- Is interesting.
- Shows deep thinking.

Self-assessment is closely related to goal setting; as students come to see the strengths and weaknesses of their work, they can set realistic, ambitious goals for their own work. In the Concept-Based classroom, students should set both short- and long-term goals related to conceptual understanding. Figure 5.18 shows one student's list of goals.

FIGURE 5.18   SAMPLE GOALS

Short-Term Goals	Long-Term Goals
• I want to make my statement more precise. • I want to find at least three examples to support my statement. • I want to learn more about the role of . . . in this situation.	• I want to use my understanding of . . . and . . . to make my community a safer place. • I want to reach the "expert" level on the rubric by myself.

Portfolios are a great way to record and track progress toward goals. At the start of a unit, teachers and students should collaborate to set goals, ensuring a mix of student-generated goals and those suggested by the teacher. Students can then collect work samples and reflections that show their progress relative to these goals.

If our ultimate goal is not just measurement, but growth, this process of assessing with clear and consistent criteria, frequent feedback, and regular reflection is imperative. When students are able to evaluate their own work against a set of clear criteria, they are empowered to take more control over their learning and decide what to do next.

Tools for Making the Goals Visible

One of the most challenging aspects of Concept-Based teaching is making the goal of learning clear without revealing "the answer" to students. We begin each unit with statements of conceptual relationship in mind, but we guide students to this understanding without telling them the statement directly.

The tools in Figure 5.19 help to make the goals visible without revealing the answer that students often mindlessly try to copy (IBO, 2000).

Figure 5.20 shows a rubric we have used in elementary classrooms with examples that illustrate responses that would receive the score shown in the column heading.

Methods to Determine Where We Are in the Learning Journey

While the tools in the previous section are useful for communicating goals to students, Figure 5.21 shows the variety of methods that can be used to track student progress toward those goals (IBO 2000). A variety of tools is particularly important to build the deep learning necessary for Concept-Based classrooms.

FIGURE 5.19   TOOLS FOR MAKING THE GOALS VISIBLE

Rubrics	Rubrics provide criteria for judging a range of student performances from poor in quality to excellent. Assessing conceptual understanding requires evaluating where students' generalizations fall on a spectrum of accuracy, adequate support, and sophistication. Rubrics can be a helpful tool in both outlining this spectrum for students and providing descriptive feedback in a way that is both efficient and effective. In an early elementary classroom, we suggest that the children, with the guidance of the teacher, develop their own rubrics. This allows children to take ownership of their learning and helps them better understand the assessment task. While developing the rubric with students, start by asking students to envision and describe the highest-quality work. This becomes the highest level on the rubric. Then ask them to think about the opposite of good work, and record these descriptors as the lowest level of the rubric. Later, the teacher can fill in the performance levels that span between these two extremes.
Exemplars / Benchmarks	These are samples of student work that have been judged against other samples. In the world of conceptual teaching and learning, this means we need to show students models of complex, insightful generalizations supported by sufficient, compelling evidence. Examples can vary from samples of writing to visual presentations and oral presentations. We want these models to inspire students and make them think, "I can create something as profound and well defended as that!" Models should be intellectual candy for students. Of course, your example shouldn't be about the conceptual relationship that students are exploring; that makes it seem like there is one right answer, and you just showed the students the back of the book. Instead, share examples of different conceptual relationships, and have students analyze what makes those examples so high quality. Sharing a model—whether student work or something we create—is powerful in both motivating students (they see what is possible) and guiding them toward the goal (instead of an abstract idea, they have a concrete example).
Checklists	These are lists of knowledge or skills that you want students to demonstrate. In an early primary setting, it is useful to keep checklists at every learning center in the classroom. You may want to address specific skills for each learning center in the classroom.
Continuums	These are visual representations of the progression of development through stages of learning. For example, in the stages of writing development, young students may move from the role-play writing stage to the early writing stage to the advanced writing stage.
	Engage students with these tools by helping them identify their place in the continuum and to build excitement about the next steps in their journey. This tool is also useful when students self-assess their understanding on a continuum. They can mark an X on a line noting where they feel they are.

FIGURE 5.20   SAMPLE CONCEPTUAL RUBRIC

1	2	3
I can explain the concepts in my own words and give an example of each.	I can explain a weak relationship between two concepts in my own words and give an accurate example.	I can explain a strong relationship between two concepts in my own words and provide powerful, clear examples that prove that relationship.
Humans are living things that can talk. For example, I am a human. Resources are things that we can use for different reasons. For example, water is a resource.	Human beings use resources. For example, people in my town use water to keep their lawns green and to bathe.	Human beings rely on resources in order to survive. For example, without water humans die in a matter of days.

Observations, Conversations, and Demonstrations in the Early Years

While assessing the growth and learning of very young children, it is important to take into consideration the child's developmental stage, background, and experiences. Assessment in the early years should be organized as part of the instruction and should be a fundamental but completely normal part of the learning in early years classes.

The *Growing Success—The Kindergarten Addendum* (2016) refers to descriptive feedback as "noticing and learning" to make the learning visible to the young child. For example, "I see that you have put farm animals in this circle and wild animals in the other circle. This is called sorting." This strategy is an efficient way to show children what and how they are learning. As the educator continues to consistently use this method of feedback, the students will have a clearer and deeper understanding of what they are learning and their next steps of learning.

Gentle observations, conversations, and demonstrations are perhaps the most powerful tools for assessing young children. The longer we can avoid stopping instruction for evaluations such as spelling tests and grades that put a numeric value on students, the better we preserve their natural curiosity. As educators continue to provide descriptive feedback and guidance, this will ultimately prepare young children to become engaged and life-long learners.

> Gentle observations, conversations, and demonstrations are perhaps the most powerful tools for assessing young children.

FIGURE 5.21 METHODS TO DETERMINE WHERE WE ARE IN THE LEARNING JOURNEY

Observations	Students are observed regularly. Observations can be taken in different situations, of whole groups, small groups, or simply observing and focusing on one child. The observations can be taken while working with the child or simply observing from the outside.
Performance assessments	This is a set performance task that is created from the generalization. The task is goal directed and is usually a transfer and application of knowledge and skills to a conceptual understanding.
Process assessments	Learning skills (such as time management, collaborative skills, self-regulations skills) are observed and recorded.
Selected responses	Tests, quizzes—this is another way of organizing data. It is important to note that administering a test in isolation may not give you the most accurate evidence of learning.
Open-ended tasks	Students are asked to justify and communicate their thinking. Answers can vary in format: written, drawn, or diagrammed.
Portfolios	Collections of students' work showing growth over time. Students can also track their growth over time within a given conceptual understanding and across their trajectory as conceptual learners. Over time, students can collect examples of work they are proud of to share either with their teacher, parents, or a panel of outside experts. Students can use work samples to defend their overall claims about their growth over time. For example, 1. Students can use anything from binders to pizza boxes to store work samples as a portfolio. 2. Students must decide on evidence to be included in their portfolios—does it show progress toward achieving goals? They should include evidence such as • Running records. • Classroom assessments. • Writing assessments. • Attitude inventories. 3. Have students organize their work with a table of contents or dividers.
Anecdotal Records	Anecdotal records are brief written notes about each child. There are many different ways of organizing these records; for example, you could write your observational notes on small sticky notes for each student and then, at the end of the school day, compile them into a more formal comment for each child's file.

Conclusion

Assessment often feels high-stakes, which can create anxiety for students, teachers, administrators, and parents. Some of our most difficult conversations and heated debates have been about assessment. While we agree that assessments are incredibly important and should be taken seriously by all stakeholders, it's imperative that we link assessments' importance and value to their purpose: understanding where students are in their learning and how they can move forward as well as what is working about our instruction and where we need to improve.

As we pursue the goal of deepening students' understanding of conceptual relationships and their ability to transfer that understanding to grapple with novel contexts, we need to be intellectually honest with ourselves, our students, and all stakeholders about the data we are gathering from assessments. That kind of honesty is not always easy, but it's vital if we want to help our students grow. We also need to be rigorous about our assessment design to ensure that our assessments are focused on what we really want to measure.

Now that you have the foundation, growing your practice will require lots of reflection, feedback from trusted colleagues, and experimentation. Mistakes are great ways to learn; that's as true for us as it is for our students! So keep the principles and examples of assessment for conceptual learning in mind, keep experimenting with personalized variations, keep pushing yourself and others to try new things, and keep reflecting on how it's all working. With that combination, we have no doubt your assessments will help your students on their journey for deep, conceptual understanding.

Chapter Review

- What is the purpose of assessment in conceptual teaching and learning?
- When during a unit should assessment take place? What types of assessment are appropriate at the beginning, middle, and end of a unit?
- How should students and teachers use the information gathered from assessments?
- What makes feedback effective?
- How can models, rubrics, student goal setting, and reflection help deepen students' conceptual understanding?

CHAPTER 6

How Can We Work Toward Equity in a Concept-Based Classroom?

This chapter will certainly not solve the enormous challenge of equity in schools, but we hope the ideas will contribute to your toolbox in this important area. The National Equity Project's website defines equity this way: "Educational equity means that each child receives what he or she needs to develop to his or her full academic and social potential" (http://nationalequityproject.org/about/equity). Gender, social class, race, language, and learning difficulties are just some of the categories that affect equity. We decided to include this chapter because conceptual learning is an important piece of equity, and we wanted to take it further with additional strategies. Although these cannot alone solve the problem of educational inequity, the principles and strategies presented here should add to the conversation.

This chapter takes the reader through four key areas that are essential for equity:

1. Teacher **expectations** and **relationship**s with students

2. Purposeful and **clear** goals, activities, instructions, and assessments

3. Constant **collection of evidence, feedback,** and **goal setting** by teacher and students

4. **Flexible grouping** based on what students **need at that moment** to reach the goal

First, it is still all too acceptable for teachers to use words like "weak students" or "smart students." This is a dangerous habit, as research shows us how easily these beliefs can be propagated and, fortunately, challenged (Dweck, 2006; Rosenthal & Jacobson, 2003). Students need to believe that their teacher is invested in their individual success (Hattie, 2012). Otherwise, instructional strategies aimed to serve the different needs of students are not likely to impact achievement. We have to *start* by challenging expectations and building relationships with students.

Second, recent research (Hattie, 2012; Marzano, 2004) supports what we have observed in countless classrooms and conversations with special educators. *Clarity* in classroom instructions and activities is an essential element for student achievement. Nearly every teacher falls victim to lack of clarity, often with the worthy goal of trying to make a learning experience "engaging." It is essential that every student understands the lesson goal and how each activity moves him or her closer to that goal.

Third, we need to be sure that assumptions are not influencing our decisions about how we group students or provide different learning experiences. Collecting *reliable data* becomes key. Preassessments tell us what students already know, understand, or misunderstand about a topic. Student goal setting, ongoing assessment, and timely, positive feedback let students know where they are in the learning journey.

Finally, once the first three prerequisites are in place, we can begin to differentiate instruction based on what students need at particular moments in the learning process. In equitable classrooms, we should see teachers who are warm yet firm in their expectations, circulating among students who are all deeply invested in a clear and purposeful task that they know will help them advance in the learning journey. The sections below provide tools and tips for each of these four areas.

> Concept-Based Curriculum is naturally more equitable than a traditional, coverage-centered curriculum.

Shifting to a conceptual learning environment, where students are guided to discover the relationships between concepts supported by facts and specific contexts, is an important step in creating equitable classrooms. Most students— especially those who traditionally do poorly in school—thrive in an environment that centers on deep understanding and the application of learning in unique ways. When we ask students to find patterns and make connections, we give them intellectual dignity.

Therefore, Concept-Based Curriculum is naturally more equitable than a traditional, coverage-centered curriculum. When facts are *organized around key concepts*, it makes them *easier to remember*. This automatically benefits students who struggle with strict memorization without context or meaning. See Figure 6.1 for a first-grade visual arts example.

Additionally, students are able to *find their own examples* that support their statements of conceptual relationship. This allows them to bring their own interests

FIGURE 6.1   VISUAL ARTS EXAMPLE

A student of visual arts learning about different artists and their corresponding works of art would be better able to memorize facts about the works if he or she discovered, through inquiry, that *different colors, shapes and lines communicate different emotions* rather than simply trying to memorize aspects about a work without this depth of understanding.

FIGURE 6.2   ILLUSTRATIONS IN STORIES EXAMPLE

Students reading stories discover, through inquiry, that *illustrations support the message of a story*. As a check for understanding, the teacher can ask each student to select a story of his or her choice and describe how an illustration supports the message.

and experiences into their learning. Faster processors can be challenged to find more examples or even examples that complicate or contradict the relationship. See Figure 6.2 for a kindergarten example for illustrations in stories.

Furthermore, we can *gradually increase the complexity* of the statements of conceptual relationship in our lesson planning, starting with less complex and scaffolding to the goal of the unit. Consider the example in Figure 6.3 for a lower elementary science unit. The two numbered statements are simpler versions of the bigger conceptual relationship taken from the kindergarten–second-grade band of the Next Generation Science Standards.

FIGURE 6.3   SCIENCE EXAMPLE

Concepts: weather, patterns, time

Statement of conceptual relationship: People measure weather conditions to describe patterns over time (NGSS, KG–2).

Scaffolded statements:

1. People measure sunlight, rain, wind, and temperatures to describe weather.
2. People notice patterns in weather.

Teachers exclaim time and time again how conceptual teaching and learning help students retain information and reach understanding on a deeper level. Organizing our curriculum around key relationships between and among concepts is the first significant step to take. The strategies below will enhance our path toward more equitable classrooms.

The Importance of Teacher Expectations and Relationships

Strategy #1: Take action to combat low expectations.

There is an overwhelming amount of research that tells us how impactful adult expectations can be on student achievement (Marzano, 2007; Rosenthal & Jacobson, 2003). It's heart-wrenching, and we almost wish we didn't have so much power over students—especially based on often-unconscious assumptions. Decades of research demonstrates that the interlocking factors of race, social class, and gender frequently lead to teachers making unconscious predictions about students (Eiland, 2008). We often mispredict what students are capable of, and this can quickly become a self-fulfilling prophecy.

One of the earliest and most famous studies on this topic was conducted by Robert Rosenthal in 1964 (Rosenthal & Jacobson, 2003). Dr. Rosenthal gave elementary students from several different classes an IQ test. He randomly selected several students and told the teachers the test predicted that these particular students were going to experience a dramatic growth in IQ. Can you guess what happened? Following these students for two years, he found that these randomly selected kids did indeed have a growth in their IQ. How did this happen? Further research revealed that nearly imperceptible interactions from the teachers were the cause of this dramatic impact, from smiling at these students more to providing them with more specific feedback.

> The key is to focus on teacher behaviors.

This research became known as the Pygmalion effect—where we subconsciously make predictions about students' abilities, often based on factors such as race and gender—and those predictions become reality. Later researchers such as Robert Pianta, dean of the Curry School at the University of Virginia (Hamre & Pianta, 2006), and Robert Marzano (2007) show that it is incredibly difficult for teachers to control their expectations of students. Both of these researchers agree that *the key is to focus on teacher behaviors.*

We like Marzano's term of *low-expectancy students,* which is different from *low-skilled* students, as it focuses on the fact that some students are *expected* to be low achievers. It then becomes more motivating and effective to think, "Let's take action to challenge the expectations of what these kids are capable of achieving and prove everyone wrong" rather than, "They need a lot more time and one-on-one attention to catch up."

At first glance, it can feel superficial or even silly to change the way we talk about students. But the research cannot be denied. Our expectations matter. Compare two ways to talk about students, as shown in Figure 6.4. While it may feel strange at first, it is worth a schoolwide effort to replace some of the language we use to discuss differences among our students. Consider long-term implications if the labels are changed into expectation–challenging language.

FIGURE 6.4   TRADITIONAL VERSUS EXPECTATION-CHALLENGING LANGUAGE

Traditional Language	Expectation-Challenging Language
Low-ability students	Low-expectancy students
Students are not able to or can't do certain tasks	Students are not ready yet or need scaffolding
Naughty, bad, or mischievous students	Spirited, funny, energetic, creative, opinionated, free-thinking students

But teacher attitudes are only one part of the picture. Parents', peers', and students' own attitudes about their likelihood to succeed also contribute to students not reaching their full potential. As we challenge our assumptions, we need to consider what we can do to challenge other people's expectations of certain students as well.

Once you've identified a few of these low–expectancy students, it's time to take action. The steps in Figure 6.5 will make a huge difference on achievement (Hamre & Pianta, 2006; Marzano, 2007; Spiegel, 2012).

FIGURE 6.5   TEACHER EXPECTATIONS AND ACTION STEPS

Action Step	Questions or Ideas to Consider
1. Make a list of students who typically perform below average, and make notes at the end of the week about your interactions with them.	• Did I joke around with this student this week? Try to do this more often. • Did I use a harsh tone or become impatient with this student more than with other students? Try not to do this. • Did I check this student's work formally and informally (e.g., over the shoulder) and give him or her positive, constructive feedback?
2. Deliberately choose one or two small actions you will take with low-expectancy students over the course of a week.	• Seat them closer to you. • Make an effort to smile at them more. • Look them in the eye more. • Lean toward them more. • Be generally more friendly and supportive. • Call on them more often. • Ask them challenging questions. • Delve into their answers deeply. • Reward them only for rigorous responses.

(Continued)

FIGURE 6.5 (Continued)

Action Step	Questions or Ideas to Consider
3. Observe low-expectancy students, listen to their conversations with peers, and ask them questions about their individual interests and how they prefer to learn.	• What are their hobbies? • What motivates them? • How do they prefer to learn?
4. Try to react to challenging behaviors with calm and empathy. Students often misbehave to try to get attention. Count to three before reacting.	• Have I given this student positive attention lately? • How can I respond first with empathy? For example, *I realize that it's hot in here today* or *I understand that you want to answer the question and that is great; you just need to wait until I call on you.*
5. Try to spend time outside of your role as teacher especially with low-expectancy students. Attend their basketball game, play games with them at recess, have a special breakfast or lunch with a small group, et cetera.	• What do these students do in their free time? • How can I engage in nonacademic activities with these students?
6. Find a way to learn about things they are interested in. Many students are skilled artists or athletes. Make note of how motivated or skilled they are in other areas of their lives.	• How does watching these students in a different context change my view of them?
7. Pay attention to signals that might tell you when certain students are having a bad day.	• What does this student's body language say today? • What might I say to this student if I notice the student is having a bad day?
8. Structure class time to allow all students to have access to challenging materials and complex thought. Don't pull kids out frequently or divide classes into groups that reflect different perceived levels of capability.	• How have I challenged low-expectancy students this week? • Do I find myself pushing the thinking of certain students over others? • Does my grouping or the school's grouping subtly or overtly label students as high or low achievers?

If you are finding students who struggle, we believe the first step is to analyze your relationship and behavior toward these students. Focus on building their self-confidence around learning using the specific behavior and reflection questions in Figure 6.5.

Clarity of Goals, Instructions, Activities, and Assessments

Strategy #2: Work on your clarity.

What do you notice about the classroom scenario in Figure 6.6?

FIGURE 6.6   EXAMPLE

Conceptual goal: The steepness of a ramp determines the speed of objects going down the ramp.

Kindergarten students are making ramps out of wooden blocks and sending cars down each one. They are working in groups of three, laughing, and seeming to enjoy themselves and the activity. Teachers offer different objects to increase the height and steepness of the ramps. Some students squeal with delight upon making a really tall ramp.

Although this might seem like an exaggeration, we have observed hundreds of classroom scenarios like the one in Figure 6.6. Although the activity is fun and hands-on, and probably has real academic value in the teacher's mind, the connection to the learning goal is often lost.

Here's an important clarification: We are huge fans of complex, messy, authentic, intellectual work. The trick is to make sure that the goal is clear and that the activity explicitly builds understanding toward the goal. And if the goal is a complex process—such as writing an argumentative essay—we try to focus on *one strategy or skill at a time.* We can layer on skills, knowledge, understanding, habits of mind, et cetera. Many students get lost in a sea of messiness when the goal is unclear.

Even if the *task* is complex, the *instructions* need to be crystal clear. Simple directions lead to complex thinking, while complex directions often lead to fragmented, simple thinking. We need to show students what quality work looks like and what weak work looks like, discussing specifically what it is lacking. Rubrics, sample student work, and think-alouds are good tools to aid us in this endeavor.

Look at the classroom example in Figure 6.7, and identify the ways in which the teacher provides clarity to her students. Contrast this with the example from Figure 6.6—what are the differences?

> Even if the *task* is complex, the *instructions* need to be crystal clear.

FIGURE 6.7 CLASSROOM EXAMPLE

The conceptual goal: Characters' feelings and actions contribute to the sequence of events in a story (CCSS.ELA-Literacy.RL.3.3).

The teacher conducted a pretest at the start of the unit to see what students knew and understood about the concepts. Based on this information, she quickly reviewed some prerequisite knowledge that most of them had already mastered as well as retaught these skills to four students who seemed to need more in-depth review.

Before she did a discovery lesson on the conceptual understanding, she wanted to be sure they understood what a successful character description looks like in general, so the next two lessons focused on that goal.

She posted a different conceptual understanding of literary devices she knew they all understood (she didn't share the exact understanding in order to allow students to discover it on their own) and conducted a think-aloud of a character description to show students what goes on in *her* mind as she describes. Students used a rubric to evaluate her description example together as a class.

In groups, the students repeated the exercise using the rubric to evaluate a weak character description (nonexample). She posted the instructions for the group work on the board, explained them aloud, and asked a student to state what they were supposed to do for the activity. Then she asked another student to explain how this activity would move them closer to mastering the goal of the unit, asked if everyone understood what they were supposed to do, clarified one student's question, and waited until 100 percent of students nodded their heads in agreement that they understood what to do before releasing them to do the group work.

The formative assessment gave students another character description, and they had to *individually* repeat the same exercise they did in their group—evaluating the strengths and weaknesses of this new description. The teacher used the individual students' evaluations to plan for the next two lessons, which explored the specific conceptual understanding, layering on this goal while also reteaching any students who needed more help on character description.

What did you identify as efforts toward clarity in this teacher's classroom? Compare your findings with those in Figure 6.8.

FIGURE 6.8 STEPS FOR CLARITY

1. Conduct a preassessment.
2. Review or reteach students who are lacking prerequisite knowledge.
3. Demonstrate what success looks like through model work and a think-aloud.
4. Utilize the rubric to evaluate strong and weak work.
5. Post instructions visually and explain them aloud. Have a student explain the instruction in his or her own words. Then respond to any questions, and wait for 100 percent comprehension before moving on. (Note: If the teacher has earned the trust of students, most students will be able to admit that they don't understand what to do— and strategies like this at least gets those who are daydreaming to focus on the lesson.)
6. Use ongoing, formative assessments to allow students to practice.
7. Use data from the formative assessments to plan instruction.

The research around clear learning goals and success criteria makes establishing goals an essential step toward achieving deep, conceptual understanding for all students (Hattie et al., 2017). If you have students who are struggling, check in with them often to ensure they understand the goal and how they are going to get there.

More and more teachers are finding English language learners in their classrooms. Clarity of goals, instructions, activities, and assessments is particularly important for English language learners. We have woven in nearly all of the research-based strategies from *Classroom Instruction That Works with English Language Learners* (Hill & Miller, 2014). These authors discussed the importance of setting objectives and providing feedback to learners, as well as allowing students to use nonlinguistic representations of their learning aligning with several strategies we have already discussed in this book. Hill and Miller also described the research behind asking students to generate and test hypotheses, which is one of our lesson frameworks from Chapter 4.

Additional strategies for English language learners:

- Identifying similarities and differences: This is particularly important when building understanding of individual concepts. By asking students to sort examples and nonexamples of concepts, we are helping English language learners develop a depth of understanding.

- Note taking: Try to use a variety of strategies for teaching students explicitly how to take notes, such as webbing or concept mapping as well as making outlines. You can also help students by using a color coding system, such as using yellow highlighters for concepts and conceptual ideas and green highlighters for factual examples or details.

Every student should be able to answer the following questions during every lesson:

- What is the **goal**?
- What **exactly** should I be doing or thinking about in this moment?
- Why are we doing this activity and how does it **directly** relate to helping me reach the goal?

Collecting and Analyzing Data

Strategy #3: Collect ongoing evidence and give inspiring feedback.

Once we have taken action toward students identified as low expectancy and spent time focused on becoming clearer on our goals, activities, and instructions, we are ready for the next step toward equitable classrooms. Chapter 5 contains specific tools for collecting ongoing, frequent evidence of individual student understanding through formative assessment. We then use this data to adjust instruction accordingly, such as reteaching certain students and providing extension activities to others.

We felt it worth repeating the importance of collecting ongoing evidence and providing feedback in this chapter on equity. We've visited hundreds of classrooms, and rarely do we see teachers and students using specific evidence to analyze their learning progress. Strategies for students analyzing their own progress, setting their own goals, and monitoring their thinking and learning along the way have led to significant improvements in achievement (Hattie et al., 2017).

> We must not confuse students' past or even current achievements with what they are ultimately capable of.

In this context, we emphasize a most important point: We must not confuse students' past or even current achievements with what they are ultimately capable of. For example, a fifth-grade student reading at the second-grade level is still very capable of complex thinking. And English language learners are capable of more complex thought in their mother tongues than they can demonstrate in English. So, while data is important in the learning journey, we must take care to constantly look to build on strengths and identify ways to draw out students' full potential. We must use more than one data point when making decisions and try to use a mixture of quantitative data and qualitative data.

When we assess, we have to be careful not to crowd an assessment item with a lot of noise that is not targeting precisely what we want to measure. For example, if recall of specific information is not important to you, add a word bank. If you don't need students to remember specific steps when asking for application, list the steps on the assessment. We also need to provide accommodations for students with specific learning difficulties. For instance, if there is a lot of text on an exam, it can be read aloud to a student with dyslexia.

For the purpose of equity, the importance of providing *specific, positive feedback* on each students' progress toward the learning goal cannot be overstated. Teachers must consider the point of view of the students and think about what information will be most useful in motivating them and moving them along in the learning process. Ask yourself, "If I were this student, what would I want to hear to help motivate me to work hard to reach the goal?" and "How can I make this feedback positive?"

For example, if a student typically has trouble writing a paragraph and the task was to write an essay, instead of saying *You are far away from writing an essay,* communicate the growth the student has made on writing a single paragraph (if that is evident in the work sample). Constantly emphasizing what the student has not yet mastered is called the deficit model—and it doesn't work in helping kids learn quickly. It is more effective to build on students' strengths.

Research on minority students attending predominately white colleges showed an incredibly powerful formula for feedback that motivates students. First, repeat the standard of excellence you are aiming to achieve. Second, point to pieces of their work that demonstrate they are capable of reaching the standard. Third, make recommendations for what to improve on next in order to move closer to the standard (Steele, 2011).

Implementing and Managing a Differentiated Classroom

Once we've actively worked on addressing our **attitudes** about students and our **clarity** in all classroom activities, and we have been collecting **evidence** of student understanding, then—and only then—are we ready for students to be working on different things at the same time in class. In addition to students working on different activities, we should also remember to vary the means of whole-group instruction, such as using visuals, audio, hands-on activities, or kinsethetic activities to increase the chances of students grasping the intended goals.

Differentiated instruction has various configurations, such as

- Individual work time on different tasks
- Heterogeneous groups of students teaching or providing feedback to each other
- Teacher conferencing with or reteaching certain students

Differentiation is about giving students *exactly* what they need at *particular moments* in the learning journey based on *ongoing evidence* collected from formative assessments. This can include extension activities beyond the target learning goal for students who are ready for more complex work.

Individuals or groups of students can be

- Reading a complex text or primary source
- Giving feedback on one another's work
- Doing practice exercises
- Taking a quiz
- Watching a video
- Listening to a podcast
- Playing an online game
- Using flash cards to build memory of key terms or ideas
- Receiving more or less scaffolding, such as sentence stems, examples, and nonexamples

Strategy #4: Steps to differentiate in a Concept-Based classroom.

Step 1. Assessment: After conducting a preassessment, you will know what different students need at the start of the unit. Figure 6.9 provides some ideas for responding to typical points of confusion.

A few typical outcomes from preassessment data include these:

- Typically, some students will need more clarification of the *concepts themselves,* while others will already have a solid grasp. For example, in science class, some students may think *equilibrium* means "equal" rather than "a balance." In social studies, some students may think of power only as formal political power and will need to expand their view.

- It is also common that some students have a *misunderstanding* of the conceptual relationship, which needs to be corrected.

- Finally, it is very typical for some students to have an *overly simplistic* understanding of the conceptual relationship. This is where you would scaffold the complexity of the statement and look for contexts that illustrate the increasing complexity.

FIGURE 6.9   RESPONDING TO ASSESSMENT DATA

Assessment Result	Possible Instructional Strategies	Example
Weak understanding of the concept(s)	• Concept attainment • Flash cards (see quizlet.com for resources) • Scenario match	Math students sort cards into examples and nonexamples of *octagons.*
Misunderstanding of the conceptual relationship	• Match relationship to examples • Make a visual map of understanding • Test hypothesis to disprove misconception	Music students match statements about the relationship between *rhythm* and *melody* to pieces of music.
Overly simplistic understanding of the conceptual relationship	• Match examples with two concepts; then describe the relationship • Ask "why," "how," or "so what" • Work down the Structure of Knowledge or Structure of Process • Peer feedback	Social studies students read examples of the relationship between *government* and *leadership* and try to identify and articulate the relationship.

Assessment Result	Possible Instructional Strategies	Example
Solid understanding of the conceptual relationship	• Introduce complications • Make own Structure of Knowledge diagram or Structure of Process diagram • Transfer to new situations • Peer teach • Provide feedback to peers	Science students transfer understanding of the relationship between *plants* and *survival* to a new, complex situation.

Step 2. Planning: When first starting differentiation, we recommend placing students in two or three groups. That will feel more manageable—but be sure that you do not reinforce low-expectancy grouping. As you become more skilled at planning for differentiation, you can plan more than three different activities. Example: One group does the concept attainment activity explained in Chapter 3, while another group begins experimenting with conceptual relationships. Consider using learning stations and giving students options.

Step 3. Execution: Unfortunately, many middle to upper elementary students are conditioned to do almost nothing without constant direction from a teacher. They usually will not immediately work well in more self-directed learning environments. Consider the tips in Figure 6.10 to establish effective use of precious class time.

FIGURE 6.10   TIPS FOR EFFECTIVE DIFFERENTIATION

Tips:	Might Look Like:
Teach students how to work effectively in groups.	• Students take three minutes to jot down what makes teamwork successful and discuss with their group. • Peer evaluation of individual teammate participation. • Teacher evaluation of participation. • Provide sentence stems to help solicit participation from reluctant or quiet students. "_____, what do you think?" • Use protocols to guide equitable collaboration. • Use group roles to help structure teamwork.

(Continued)

FIGURE 6.10 (Continued)

Tips:	Might Look Like:
Teach students how to work independently and to keep going even when they feel stuck. (We've witnessed way too much wasted class time while students sit and wait for the teacher to finish conferencing with another group.)	• Classroom rule: You cannot stop work while waiting for the teacher, move on to something else, or just try to move forward before getting help. • Create a norm where students have to ask three students for help before asking the teacher. • Give hypothetical scenarios, and discuss how students can move on even while waiting for the teacher. • Use some sort of simple signal—like putting a card with a question mark face-up on the desk—so the teacher knows you need help.
Utilize the rubric and student goal setting so they know why they are working on what they are working on at that moment.	• Students glue the rubric to the inside cover of their notebook and refer to it every day for reflection. • Students identify one area where they've improved to celebrate success.
Mix teacher-directed activities with student choice.	• Some days, explain the different learning activities or stations, and let students choose what makes the most sense given where they are in the learning journey.
Conference with students regularly.	• Listen to students; try to figure out from them how you can help them learn better.
Reteach or provide minilessons when students need them.	• If you notice a majority of students in small groups are misunderstanding a key point, pull attention to the front of the room to reexplain to everyone at the same time, rather than going group to group to reexplain the same thing. • During small group or one-on-one sessions, ask a lot of questions, and allow students to admit areas of confusion and construct meaning for themselves in this more private space.
Collect and save your materials.	• Laminate images or other materials to be used over and over again. • Different groups can use the same materials on different days. • It is likely that the concepts and examples will resurface throughout the school year.

Tips:	Might Look Like:
Be sure to vary the groups! If you find yourself keeping students in the same groups (particularly if they can be viewed as "slower" and "faster" groups) for more than a few lessons, then it's time to work harder on taking action toward low-expectancy students.	• Talk with students who still seem to be struggling after a couple days to brainstorm together ways to support them. • Include independent work regularly, even for just a few minutes. • Play games with mixed groups. • Use different activities that allow different students to shine (e.g. drawing, callisthenic activity outside).

Tips for Inclusive Classrooms

It is common practice to pair a special educator with a teacher in many classrooms, but we have found that few schools provide structures or training for effective use of this arrangement. It can often feel like the subject teacher is "in charge," and the special educator is more like an aide than an equal partner. We've also seen many teachers view the special educator as the one to solve the "problems" with students who learn differently. This should not be the case.

The goal of the relationship between a general educator and a special educator is to build the general educator's own capacity in reaching all students. The special educator should be working to coach the general educator on strategies and when to employ them. Their collaboration could rotate between coplanning, offering feedback, and modeling lesson plans for students. After a few coplanning sessions, the general education teacher should have collected enough strategies to be able to plan for accommodations on his or her own, without the special educator present.

In order to facilitate coplanning based on the principles in this chapter, we've created a potential list of questions to use during coplanning sessions. It is shown in Figure 6.11.

FIGURE 6.11   QUESTIONS TO FACILITATE COPLANNING FOR INCLUSIVE CLASSROOMS

Questions to Facilitate Coplanning for Inclusive Classrooms
• What is the learning goal for the day? If it is a complex process, which strategy or skill are we focused on for this lesson? • How will students know what quality work looks like? • How does each learning activity move students toward that goal? • How will we ensure the instructions for each activity are clear and understood? • How will we collect evidence on whether or not individual students are on track toward achieving the goal? • How well do our formative and summative assessments measure precisely what it is we want to measure?

(Continued)

FIGURE 6.11 (Continued)

Questions to Facilitate Coplanning for Inclusive Classrooms
• How will we give positive and specific feedback to students all along the learning journey process?
• How will we provide support for those who need extra help?
• How will we show increased attention to low-expectancy students (e.g., smile more, use their names more, give more feedback, get to know them personally)?

Teacher Self-Assessment for Equitable Classrooms

A deep commitment to equity is an important goal, especially in today's diverse classrooms. We frequently use the self-assessment in Figure 6.12 to reflect on our own practice and try to identify ways to improve. Try it out and see where you might want to focus your efforts.

FIGURE 6.12 TEACHER SELF-ASSESSMENT ON EQUITABLE CLASSROOMS

Teacher Self-Assessment on Equitable Classrooms	
How well do I employ the following teaching strategies?	Circle a number from 1 to 4, where 1 represents *never* and 4 represents *daily*.
Attitudes and Expectations of Students	
I choose low-expectancy students and focus on giving more attention, smiles, feedback, and praise.	1 2 3 4
Clarity of Goals, Activities, and Instructions	
Students have a clear picture of what quality work looks like and what they need to do to achieve the goal.	1 2 3 4
My learning activities always clearly move students toward the learning target.	1 2 3 4
My instructions for each activity are simple and clear.	1 2 3 4
Collecting Evidence and Giving Feedback to Students	
My assessments clearly measure the precise learning target and do not contain any unnecessary "noise."	1 2 3 4
I collect individual evidence of student understanding.	1 2 3 4
I give individual, positive, and effective feedback to students about where they are in the learning journey.	1 2 3 4

Teacher Self-Assessment on Equitable Classrooms	
Differentiated Activities	
I modify instruction based on data collected showing where students are in the learning journey.	1 2 3 4
Students work in flexible groups, individually or with me based on what they need at that moment—I do not use fixed homogeneous groups.	1 2 3 4

Conclusion

This chapter provides a few principles and strategies to move toward creating a more equitable learning environment for all students. We must constantly remind ourselves of the enormous power we have as teachers. We need to get in the habit of consistently checking our expectations of students and working toward building solid relationships with each of them, especially those who do not typically do well in school. Through positive interactions, clear instructions, and solid use of data to inform flexible grouping, we can help all students reach their potential.

Chapter Review

- What is the relationship between teacher expectations and equity? What might you say to a peer the next time you hear something like "my weak student"?
- How does clarity of goals, activities, instructions, and assessments foster equity?
- What role does evidence collecting, feedback, and goal setting have in equitable classrooms?
- Why are flexible groups essential for equitable classrooms? What does fixed grouping communicate to students?

....

How Can Conceptual Understanding Help to Preserve a Love of Learning Beyond Childhood?

> When we adults think of children there is a simple truth that we ignore: Childhood is not preparation for life; childhood is life. A child isn't getting ready to live; a child is living. (Taylor, 1993, p. 45)

The underlying philosophy throughout this book is one of honoring children's intellectual capabilities in a way that respects natural methods of making meaning. It can be easy to succumb to the pressure of preparing our students for "what's next" to the point that we forget the importance of enjoying the pleasures of childhood. We are advocates of a well-written curriculum, but we want to be clear that it must be done in a way that preserves the natural love of learning. As the final chapter of a book aimed toward younger students, we have included principles and strategies to show how conceptual understanding can aid in this important endeavor.

Forces That Erode Curiosity and Risk Taking

Babies learn everything—walking, talking, eating, et cetera—through an unabashed process of failures and literal missteps. Their fearlessness and determination are essential for their development. We need to remember that curiosity and risk taking are innate. They are not *learned* but are often *unlearned* as children grow.

Despite different positions on when and how children should be introduced to academic topics and concepts, there is no denying that as they age, students tend to lose their motivation for learning in formal schooling. Most second graders are likely to shoot their hands in the air, desperate for the teacher to call on them. This behavior is virtually nonexistent in eighth-grade classrooms. The reasons this happens are complex and include biological as well as social factors. But common schooling habits do much to harm the natural love of learning.

It is important to note and understand that part of the reason is developmental. Very young children are so egocentric they do not typically concern themselves in comparisons of skills. At around six or seven years old, they start to compare themselves to others and focus on those who are more skilled than they are in specific areas (Levine, 2014). Self-consciousness and concern for others' opinions steadily increase through adolescence. This makes a culture of a supportive community and cooperative learning incredibly important. Cooperative learning has been shown to be much more effective than competitive approaches (Hattie, 2012).

> Common schooling habits do much to harm the natural love of learning.

Another related developmental change is a shift in concern from adults' opinions to peers' opinions of themselves. As children gain a greater sense of self and control of their worlds, they typically become less concerned for adult approval and begin to question rules and norms set by the adults closest to them (Eccles & Wigfield, 2002). We can attend to this change by ensuring we build positive relationships with all of our students and establish credibility with them, both of which have been shown to produce enormous impact on student achievement (Hattie, 2012).

Perhaps most alarming is recent research into the role of external rewards and punishments in eroding intrinsic motivation (Pink, 2011). It is terrifying to watch how quickly students shift their motivation to grades and away from the joy of learning. As outlined throughout this book, we believe there should be a giant overhaul in the culture of testing. At the least, we must be extra cautious not to use tests or evaluation systems to motivate students. Consider the seemingly subtle differences between the approaches shown in Figure 7.1, and reflect on the impact of each after repeated exposure.

Above all, our concern lies with the increase of memorization and facts without a conceptual framework as students move through school. Grit and resilience are incredibly trendy terms at the moment. But we must be careful that we don't misinterpret these initiatives with a focus on building students' endurance through a curriculum design that is demotivating. The brain naturally seeks pattern recognition and meaning making. And conceptual understanding allows for organization and better retention of factual information. Explicit formulation of a conceptual framework built through an inductive teaching approach will do wonders in protecting curiosity and risk taking in schools.

FIGURE 7.1   IMPROVING LEARNING INTENTIONS

Not So Inviting Learning Intentions	More Inviting Learning Intentions
We have a test on Friday, so we need to review place value.	I was thinking about our work together, and I noticed that many of us still need to think about place value. We should spend some time reviewing place value so that we know how to determine which number is greater.
By the end of the lesson, you will be able to solve inequalities with rational numbers.	Remember all of the learning we did with inequalities? We really mastered that content as a class. Now it would be interesting to examine how to solve inequalities that were more complex, maybe with several variables. And then we could graph them to visualize what is happening. I know that several of you find it helpful in understanding when we create visual representations.
Today we are going to continue our work with statistics. We will focus our learning on scatter plots for bivariate measurement data so that we can see if there are patterns of association.	Have you ever wondered if the relationship between two things was really significant? For example, I was wondering if the number of students in a class was related to their overall scores on a test. I'm sure you all can think of things you'd like to compare. Remember, we learned that correlations don't mean cause, but that there is a relationship with the numbers. Today, we get to explore scatter plots as one tool to look for associations.

SOURCE: Hattie, J., Fisher, D., Frey, N., Gojak, L., Moore, S., & Mellman, W. (2017).

Here's a quick example for students learning to read in kindergarten or first grade. Let's say we want students to monitor their thinking as they read. We can say, "Students, it's important to monitor what's going on in our heads as we read." Or, we can use Concept-Based Curriculum and Instruction to write a statement of conceptual relationship, such as "Good readers monitor their thinking while they read." Next we can pose a question to students, such as *What do good readers think about as they read?* Or *How can we use our brains to get better at reading?* Next, we can model our thinking as we read to illustrate the point. Even better, we can create a dramatic story that shows a reader who monitors their thinking and one who does not, and ask students to compare the two. This method allows students to *uncover* the idea that *good readers monitor their thinking while they read.*

Using Conceptual Understanding to Build Social and Emotional Intelligence

Although a mountain of research demonstrates the importance of increasing students' social and emotional intelligence (Duckworth, 2016; Dweck, 2006; Wagner, 2015) a recent study tells us that *how* we do it matters a lot. In a report entitled *Hard Thinking on Soft Skills*, the Brookings Institute tells us, "Without specificity at the level of what students need to learn and examples of how to teach it, there is no clear path to the development of curriculum and instructional practices, teacher training, or meaningful assessment and accountability" (Whitehurst, 2016). We need clarity and a coherent curriculum design for these habits of mind and skills. Erickson and Lanning's curriculum model offers a sound solution here as well.

We can use the same simple approach we outlined in Chapter 3 of this book:

1. Identify conceptual relationships.

2. Turn them into conceptual questions that we present to students.

3. Create learning experiences and contexts that illustrate the relationship between the concepts.

The cycle is summarized in Figure 7.2.

FIGURE 7.2   THE CONCEPTUAL INQUIRY CYCLE

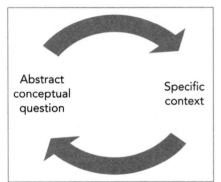

Using the work of prominent psychologists and other experts, we can develop conceptual relationships and corresponding questions for rigorous social and emotional learning. Figure 7.3 demonstrates sample relationships and questions for a curriculum design that can be built throughout elementary school. Note that Erickson allows us to bend the "no pronoun" rule, as young children can first generalize about their own lives, and then we can help them to make the connection to "people" in more abstract terms.

Choosing which ideas to emphasize requires an in-depth knowledge of the latest research on soft skills. For example, a recent publication (Bloom, 2016) demonstrates research into the importance of teaching compassion over empathy. The University of California, Berkeley's Greater Good Science Center (Compassion, n.d.), distinguished the two emotions this way:

> Compassion literally means "to suffer together." Among emotion researchers, it is defined as the feeling that arises when you are confronted with another's suffering and feel motivated to relieve that suffering. Compassion is not the same as empathy or altruism, though the concepts are related. While empathy refers more generally to our ability to take the perspective of and feel the emotions of another person, compassion is when those feelings and thoughts include the desire to help.

Empathy has been an important skill in both English language arts and social studies. But Bloom (2016) argues that empathy could lead to tribal and biased judgment when it came time for moral and political decisions. Compassion on the other hand leads to better feelings and kinder behavior toward others. Bloom asserts that a focus on compassion could make the world a better place.

FIGURE 7.3   SAMPLE CONCEPTUAL RELATIONSHIPS AND QUESTIONS

Conceptual Relationships	Corresponding Questions
Difficult situations help us to learn and grow.	What is the role of difficult situations in our learning and growth?
Becoming more conscientious and aware of our actions allows us to make better choices.	What is the relationship between awareness of our actions and the quality of our choices?
We can calm ourselves when emotions get big.	What happens when we experience big emotions?
Becoming more aware of our big emotions allows us to understand and overcome them.	What is the purpose of awareness of our big emotions in overcoming them?
Being kind to others makes me feel good.	What is the relationship between how I treat others and how I feel?
Focusing on the positive leads to a happier, healthier life.	What is the role of positivity in my life?
When things don't go our way, we don't give up; we keep trying.	What happens when things don't go our way?
Learning something new produces positive feelings.	What is the relationship between learning something new and how I feel?
Mastery requires patience and persistence and builds my self-esteem and motivation.	How do we build expertise or mastery? What role does it play in my self-esteem and motivation?
Knowledge about the world makes life more interesting.	What role does knowledge about the world play in my life?
Mistakes and failures provide information to help us learn and get smarter.	What effect do mistakes and failures have on learning?
When we step out of our comfort zones, we discover insights that are more meaningful and long lasting.	Why is it important to step out of our comfort zones when learning?
We can develop our abilities through hard work, strategies, and mentoring from others.	How can we develop our abilities?
Through hard work, I improve the quality of my thinking.	How can we develop the quality of our thinking?

(Continued)

FIGURE 7.3   (Continued)

Conceptual Relationships	Corresponding Questions
A supportive community makes learning easier and more fun.	How does our community impact our learning?
Diversity leads to creativity and innovation.	What is the role of diversity in creativity and innovation?
Violence almost always leads to more violence.	What impact does violence have on society?
I can defend myself and others with powerful words and nonviolent actions.	How can I defend myself and others?

Once we've developed statements of conceptual relationships with corresponding questions, we can move to providing examples that will illustrate the relationship between the concepts and answer the conceptual questions. It is a good idea to start with other characters and what we can learn from them, and then move toward real people in our students' lives, and then finally the students themselves. Role-play when students are calm in a fun, relaxed atmosphere rather than waiting until a conflict or undesirable behavior arises.

> Role-play when students are calm in a fun, relaxed atmosphere rather than waiting until a conflict or undesirable behavior arises.

For instance, let's say a kindergarten class has the following conceptual relationship as its goal: "Being kind to others makes me feel good." We would pose a conceptual question for students such as *What is the relationship between how I treat others and how I feel?* We could start by sharing a simple story like *Llama Llama Time to Share* (Dewdney, 2012) and asking the students what Llama learned during the story. They might say something like "Sharing and playing with others can be more fun than playing alone" or "It's fun to make new friends." We could ask them guiding questions, such as *How do you think Llama felt when he made a new friend?* This line of questioning could eventually help them to answer our abstract conceptual question: "What is the relationship between how I treat others and how I feel?" The next step is to transfer their understanding to a more complex context, such as a more complicated story line. They should eventually be able to come up with answers close to our conceptual goal: "Being kind to others makes me feel good." See Figure 7.4 for a list of sample contexts with corresponding examples.

We hope these examples sparked your thinking about how you could use conceptual understanding to foster social and emotional learning. All too often we "tell" children these big ideas without allowing them to uncover them through guided

FIGURE 7.4 SAMPLE CONTEXTS

Sample Contexts	Examples
Books	*The Quiltmaker's Gift* by Jeff Brumbeau
Videos	Everyday Speech videos (explicit) Super Friends (implicit—Mistakes and failures provide information to help us learn and get smarter)
Role-plays	Ms. Denise and I are going to act out a little scene about a little boy who didn't learn fractions on the first try. What is he going to do next? After we do it, we will assign roles and you can act it out.
Teacher-created stories	One day, there was a little girl who always focused on the negative parts of her life. She met a friend who showed her how to look for the positive things and to be thankful for what you have. . . .
Real scenarios from teachers, parents, and other adults	One time I got really frustrated and wanted to scream, but then I took a deep breath, counted to three. . . .
Real scenarios with the students themselves	When you shared your book with Lucy, how do you think it made her feel? Did it make you feel good to make another person happy?

inquiry. All people, including children, seek to make meaning for themselves for learning that lasts, and conceptual understanding serves us here as well.

Fostering Independence and Internal Motivation

It can be scary to learn that external rewards and punishments are shown to decrease internal motivation for complex tasks, as so much of schooling is designed with the carrots and sticks approach. It can be difficult to break habits, work around mandatory policies, and figure out alternatives. We thought it might be helpful to share a few ideas to help guide your Concept-Based Curriculum implementation.

Moving to a curriculum aimed at conceptual goals is an important step in fostering internal motivation. At the 2015 Future of Learning Institute, David Perkins advocated for abstracting to the conceptual level as key for engagement:

> We should be moving away from an understanding of something—the information on the test, the list of state of capitals—to an understanding with something. With the latter, students are able to then make connections to other things. For example, rather than just learning facts about the French Revolution, students should learn

about the French Revolution as a way to understand issues like world conflict or poverty or the struggle between church and state. (Hough, 2015)

Without those connections, Perkins says he's not surprised that disengaged students are raising their hands, asking why they need to know something. Done well, a Concept-Based Curriculum should inspire students to continue looking for connections between examples that will push and enrich their understanding.

> Done well, a Concept-Based Curriculum should inspire students to continue looking for connections between examples that will push and enrich their understanding.

We can further foster independence by asking students to come up with their own questions for inquiry. Figure 7.5 contains a list of ideas for what makes a high-quality question along with a few question-stems to help them generate some ideas.

You can use the criteria to show examples and nonexamples for students to evaluate. Figure 7.6 has a few examples to illustrate the point. Show the questions, and ask students if they are high or low quality.

Daniel Pink and Carol Dweck are two researchers who offer incredible insight into the factors that can help us to build our students' internal motivation for learning. Pink (2011) found that external rewards work in boosting performance if the tasks

FIGURE 7.5　CRITERIA FOR A HIGH-QUALITY QUESTION

Criteria for a High-Quality Question
- Open-ended, not closed
- Shouldn't be too easy to answer
- Focused, not too broad
- Connected to key concepts and conceptual ideas
- Interesting to me
- Will lead me to quality information
- Will lead to more questions
- Requires a variety of sources to answer well
- Requires multiple points of view or perspective to get a rounded view
- Demonstrates a common tension about life

Question Stems:
What are the pros and cons of _____?
What are the responsibilities of _____?
What is the difference between _____ and _____?
Should _____? Why or why not?

FIGURE 7.6   EXAMPLES OF HIGH-QUALITY AND LOW-QUALITY QUESTIONS

Concept: Migration

Low-quality: How many Mexicans migrate to the United States? What is the definition of migration?

High-quality: **What are the pros and cons** of migration? **What are the responsibilities** of citizenship? **What is the difference** between a migrant and a refugee? **Should** countries take in refugees fleeing war or natural disasters. . . .**Why or why not**?

are basic, mechanical skills. They work for simple problems with a single answer and an exact procedure to follow. But when a task requires more creative or higher-order thinking, they actually make performance worse.

This distinction is incredibly important for teachers to consider. Sometimes, we want students to perform basic tasks. In those cases, it seems like external rewards including stickers and other prizes can be effective. But when tasks are more complex, such as determining the relationship between two or more concepts, we are best to avoid these types of rewards.

What are we to do instead? Pink asserts that there are three areas that drive motivation: mastery, autonomy, and purpose. Mastery is the urge to improve in specific areas. Celebrating progress and helping students to "best themselves" are ways in which we can help students to experience this sense of mastery. Autonomy is the desire to be self-directed. Helping students to know themselves as learners, and giving them more independence to decide when and how to pursue learning goals, are great ways to build this area. Purpose is the desire to do something that has meaning and is important. Throughout this book, we assert that schools can help students to make a difference in the world through their learning as well as building community within schools and classrooms. These are important aspects in helping students feel their learning has value.

We can help to foster intrinsic motivation by avoiding the strategies in Figure 7.7. Think about examples of each and how they erode motivation. For example, we have seen students label themselves as "basic" or "proficient" based on standardized test scores. We have to help them see beyond test results and show them their potential.

On the other hand, there are several things we can do to foster intrinsic motivation. If you haven't already tried it, consider partnering your class with another class of students a grade

FIGURE 7.7   EXTERNAL MOTIVATION STRATEGIES TO AVOID

Avoid
competition
class rankings
labels
rewards and punishments for complex tasks
using grades or tests as motivation for learning

FIGURE 7.8 STRATEGIES TO USE TO FOSTER INTRINSIC MOTIVATION

Use
celebration of progress
students "best" themselves
present work to a public audience
get to know themselves as learners
reciprocal teaching
choice and independence on when and how to pursue goals
build community
learning that has meaning and impact beyond classroom walls
stories of successful people who failed several times on their way to success
The Learning Challenge

level a couple years older or younger than yours. Have them read to one another or work together on a project. This is a magical motivator.

Take a look at the ideas in Figure 7.8, and think about ways you could incorporate these ideas into your teaching practice.

Author James Nottingham has created something called the Learning Challenge (2017) that has been shown to foster students' internal motivation. The Learning Challenge includes four stages:

1. Introduce a **concept.**
2. **Challenge** students' initial understanding of the concept, leading them into the "learning pit."
3. **Construct** meaning, reconciling any cognitive conflicts that might exist.
4. **Consider** the learning journey.

Nottingham says that when students are in the learning pit, they have a set of unresolved ideas or contradictions that they are trying to work out. In this scenario, the goal is for students to *willingly* enter the learning pit and to see wrestling with conflicting ideas as a fun exercise that leads to deeper understanding. Again, Concept-Based Curriculum and Instruction complements this model.

We find we often use this model in our own classrooms—where we start off with a simple idea and perhaps take students through a couple contexts to illustrate the point. And then, because the world is complex, we can usually introduce a contradictory idea. For example, first-grade students could come to understand that typically, artists use soft colors and curvy lines to bring about calm emotions in painting and artwork, while they use bright colors and sharper lines to create stronger emotions such as happiness or anger. After students are feeling relatively comfortable with this idea, we can introduce work that contradicts or complicates this understanding and have them discuss their reactions. We often try to think about tensions at the outset of the unit that will draw students into a deeper understanding of the concepts, such as the tensions between individual freedom and the collective good for the community, or the tension between human needs and wants and the protection of the environment.

Helping to preserve intrinsic motivation of learning can be difficult in very traditional settings, especially with pressure from parents, administration, or government policies to "perform" on academic exams. But chances are, if you are reading this book, you are already on the path to helping students keep their natural love of learning. When we become conscious of our everyday methods for attempting to motivate students, we can see more clearly which things we should *stop* doing and which things to *start* doing.

Developing Students' Passions

A major aspect of internal motivation derives from loving what you are doing. Is it possible to allow children to deeply experience childhood while also building the foundation for successful careers in the future? We think so.

Perhaps the best way to lay the foundation for a happy adulthood is by fostering students' self-awareness and agency at a young age. The book *Well-Being* (Rath & Harter, 2010) says that career well-being may be the most important aspect of well-being. Their research shows that people with high career well-being are more than twice as likely to be thriving in their lives overall.

Career well-being can be defined as liking what you do every day. Another popular way of describing this idea is in "discovering your passion" or pursuing a career that gives you great satisfaction. The idea of discovering one's passion and purpose in life is a hot topic at the moment—but there are few resources to help people to find or develop it. The work of Ken Robinson (Robinson & Aronica, 2009, 2013) provides an incredibly useful framework and straightforward exercises largely aimed toward adults. We have included his framework in this book and adapted his ideas for educators of young children.

First, discovering and developing one's passion is a deeply personal journey; we cannot discover it *for* children. We can only provide experiences that will help them to discover and develop it on their own. An important part of the journey, Robinson notes, is questioning the things you think you are good at or not good at and trying them again. Second, we must be careful not to portray the idea that our passion is "hidden" and we suddenly "find" it. A natural aptitude is an important aspect in Robinson's framework, but he is careful to note the importance of effort and practice in order to develop our passions.

We must, **must**, *must* avoid labeling children, asserting our values for what a good passion or career pursuit might be, or pushing them in a particular direction. Some students will know they want to be a fireman at seven years old and will go on to be a fireman. But the vast majority should simply explore their likes and dislikes and build the foundation that will allow them to continue to explore and develop their passions as young adults.

Robinson makes two important distinctions that we need to make clear to students.

1. **Cultivating passion is different from "following" your passion.** Passions require deliberate effort, planning, work, and encouragement.

2. **Passion is different from preference, talent, or enthusiasm.** Passion moves beyond initial aptitude and excitement toward deep fulfillment. Passions are rooted in strong beliefs, significant impact, and a craftsman-like honing of skill.

Robinson (Robinson & Aronica, 2009) echoes Daniel Pink's research on mastery and autonomy when he says that we must believe that our lives are unique and that we create our own lives. This relates directly to growth mindsets in helping students to believe that they can improve in their abilities through effort. We have taken the work of Robinson, Pink, and Dweck to create the following five categories for educators to consider in helping students find their passions:

- Self-awareness and agency
- Experiences and opportunities
- Creativity and nontraditional intelligence
- Purpose, values, and community
- Well-being and positive mindsets

If students are supposed to believe that their lives are unique and that they can create their own lives, they need to develop their **self-awareness and agency**. We believe this is the most important of the categories in working with young children. We can increase self-awareness by regularly asking students to engage in self-assessment of their work, reflecting on their learning and the learning process, and even occasionally engaging in personality tests. Robinson cautions us, however, to challenge the results of these tests, helping students to see that they can change their interests, talents, and even habits of their personality if they choose. To foster agency, we can regularly ask students to engage in public communication, service-learning, and goal setting, and give them choice in the learning process.

> If students are supposed to believe that their lives are unique and that they can create their own lives, they need to develop their *self-awareness and agency.*

To discover their passions, students obviously need to be exposed to a variety of **experiences and opportunities**. These can include field trips, career exploration, cross-cultural exchanges, stories, videos, and images of faraway places. When we vary the learning environment with individual and group learning, callisthenic activities, hands-on creating, and technology integration, we help students have a variety of experiences. It's even better when we ask them to reflect on these different experiences to see if they might prefer working with their hands, moving their bodies, thinking individually for long periods of time, et cetera.

In order to change the traditional school norms of a narrow view of intelligence and ways of thinking, we need to work hard to promote **creativity and a diverse outlook on intelligence**. Taking this category a step further, we should intentionally push the boundaries of a traditional, academic view of intelligence. We can ask students to complete open-ended projects, conduct mind maps, and use divergent thinking. We should also ensure they are exposed to a multitude of areas such as art, dance, cooking, caring for others, organizing things, et cetera. For example, if a student finds he is particularly good at and enjoys rearranging the classroom and keeping it organized, he may become a very passionate architect, interior designer, or even consultant on home organization.

Both Pink and Robinson point out that humans need to be a part of something larger than themselves. Therefore, it is important that teachers consider promoting **purpose, values, and community** in schools. We can do this through community service projects, a gentle awareness of issues in the community (perhaps avoid war and violent conflict in the early years, but, for example, discuss pollution and protecting habitats for plants and animals). Even young children can have conversations about fairness and positive character traits.

Finally, **well-being and positive mindsets** help to round out our categories to ensure that students' pursuits of their passions are done in a healthy way. We can promote eating well, exercise, and adequate sleep with our students and their parents. Some schools have replaced punitive discipline with mindfulness and even yoga with amazing results (Khorsandi, 2016).

The self-assessment in Figure 7.9 provides an opportunity for teachers to reflect on which categories they are addressing often and which might need more emphasis. The list is certainly not exhaustive, so be sure to think about other ways you are promoting or can promote these categories with your students. The goal is to include a diversity of strategies for each section. For example, you may regularly ask students to self-assess—but a top score in that category would include regular use of *several* ideas from that section.

Reflecting on the areas in the self-assessment is a good first step to ensuring the foundation is in place to help students discover and pursue their passions. Many ideas throughout this book are aligned to the categories above, such as building a community of learners outlined in Chapter 2, and using formative assessments and goal-setting strategies described in Chapter 5. There is literally no end to the number of creative ways you could help students build these areas. But the first section of self-awareness and agency is the most important. Therefore, we've included some additional strategies in this area that might be helpful to consider.

FIGURE 7.9 CULTIVATING PASSIONS SELF-ASSESSMENT FOR TEACHERS

Cultivating Passion—Teacher Self-Assessment				
How often do I provide opportunities for my students to build these skills or mindsets?	Circle a number from 1 to 4, where 1 represents *never* and 4 represents *daily*.			
Self-Awareness and Agency				
self-assessment, critical thinking, reflecting on learning, personality tests, learning preferences, aptitude inventory	1	2	3	4
public communication, persuasion, goal setting, service-learning, leadership skills, choice	1	2	3	4
Experiences and Opportunities				
field trips, cultural exchange, career exploration, foreign language learning, internships, community interaction	1	2	3	4
nontraditional ways of learning: hands-on activities, calisthenics, conceptual understanding, disciplinary thinking	1	2	3	4
Creativity and Nontraditional Intelligence				
mind maps, divergent thinking, what-if scenarios, open-ended projects, visual displays, building, crafting	1	2	3	4
art, dance, music, sports, cooking, leading, engineering, design, caring for others, organizing	1	2	3	4
Purpose, Values, and Community				
issue awareness, community service, advocacy, ethics, philosophy, spiritual exploration, character building	1	2	3	4
Well-Being and Positive Mindsets				
meditation, exercise, eating well, mindfulness, importance of sleep, stress reduction, social/emotional learning	1	2	3	4
growth mindset, encouraging and rewarding effort, long-term projects, culture of risk taking, intellectual growth	1	2	3	4

Strategies for Building Self-Awareness and Agency

While a lot of what children enjoy is developmental (I don't think my two-year-old will *always* be obsessed with cars and trucks . . .), it is important for students to become self-aware of what they take pleasure in doing. Use the chart in Figure 7.10 to jump-start ideas for increasing self-awareness and agency. We recommend selecting

FIGURE 7.10   IDEAS FOR BUILDING SELF-AWARENESS AND AGENCY

Idea	Examples
Self-assessment	• How well do you know this word? (never heard it before—heard of it—can tell what it means)
	• Which part of this process do you think needs more practice?
• Reflecting on their learning	• How did your thinking improve today?
	• What did you learn today?
• Public communication	• Invite the principal in for a presentation.
	• Have students attend the parent-teacher association meeting and present ideas.
	• Invite older or younger students in to listen to a presentation.
• Service-learning • Ensure it is integrated with learning goals and that a significant reflection is included.	• Partner with an environmental group for a project.
	• Mentor younger students in reading development.
	• Partner with a hospital or retirement home to make art (including singing, drama, visuals).
• Goal setting	• How many words do you want to learn this week?
	• How many laps do you want to run around the playground?
	• Which concept do you want to explore deeper?
• Choice in learning	• Create learning stations from which students can choose activities (e.g., watching videos, using hands-on activities, reading quietly, working with the teacher, etc.)
	• How would you like to show your understanding of this concept? (e.g., use modeling clay to illustrate it, draw it, explain it orally with words, act it out)

just one or two to make a regular, daily habit in your classroom. After a couple weeks, begin playing with other ideas. Don't forget to combine these activities with exposing students to a variety of experiences and opportunities.

As an additional tool, in Figures 7.11 and 7.12 we show an activity we've adapted from *Finding Your Element* (Robinson & Aronica, 2013). It can be used with upper elementary students to help them become aware of the things they do well and the things they enjoy. For younger students, adults may need to ask them orally to think about and maybe draw the things that come easily to them. Teachers can read the ideas in the figure aloud to help them think about it. We can also pay attention to and monitor their likes and aptitudes. This could be a great thing to include in reporting home and collaborating with parents on identifying students' interests and capacities.

FIGURE 7.11   APTITUDE TRACKER

Circle the things that come easily to you—these are not things you are "good at" because getting good at something takes time and practice. These are just things that seem to come to you easily, maybe even in comparison to some of your peers. Scratch out the things that don't come easily to you, and write them in one of the other two columns on the right. This list is only a few ideas; feel free to write other things that seem to come easily to you in the space below the text.

Things that come fairly easily to me:	Things that are neither easy nor hard:	Things that are hard for me:
• Making new friends, being social • Numbers, quantitative reasoning • Language • Arts, painting, crafting • Imagination, acting • Solving a mystery • Understanding how things work • Music or dancing • Cooking or tasting food • Organizing my room • Organizing a party or event • Making connections between things • Sports or athletics • Physical coordination • Making an argument • Convincing people • Influencing others • Technology • Creativity—thinking differently about things • Coming up with new ideas • Making things look nice • Breaking things down into steps or parts • Caring for others • Staying calm in tense situations • Solving conflicts • Understanding the feelings of others • Making tough decisions • Communicating • Fashion, putting together an outfit, shopping		

FIGURE 7.12 ENJOYMENT TRACKER

Things that I enjoy:	Things that I neither enjoy nor dislike:	Things that I don't like doing:
Now take the same list and try to think about things you enjoy doing. Just because something is easy for you doesn't mean you necessarily enjoy it. And if you enjoy doing something, even if it's not necessarily easy for you, perhaps with lots of practice you will get good at it because you like doing it. This list is only a few ideas; feel free to write other things that you enjoy in the space below the text.		
• Making new friends, being social		
• Numbers, quantitative reasoning		
• Language		
• Arts, painting, crafting		
• Imagination, acting		
• Solving a mystery		
• Understanding how things work		
• Music or dancing		
• Cooking or tasting food		
• Organizing my room		
• Organizing a party or event		
• Making connections between things		
• Sports or athletics		
• Physical coordination		
• Making an argument		
• Convincing people		
• Influencing others		
• Technology		
• Creativity—thinking differently about things		
• Coming up with new ideas		
• Making things look nice		
• Breaking things down into steps or parts		
• Caring for others		
• Staying calm in tense situations		
• Solving conflicts		
• Understanding the feelings of others		
• Making tough decisions		
• Communicating		
• Fashion, putting together an outfit, shopping		

Concept-Based Curriculum and Instruction is not only for academic learning. The list below provides a simple three-step model to come up with a plan for helping to protect a lifelong love of learning and finding passions.

1. Identify conceptual relationships: *Developing our passions requires trying lots of new things and reflecting on things we enjoy.*

2. Turn them into conceptual questions that we present to students. *What is the role of reflecting on our lives in finding our passions?*

3. Create learning experiences and contexts that illustrate the relationship between the concepts. *Use the activities and ideas in Figures 7.12 and 7.13 to illustrate the conceptual relationship.*

Conclusion

Teaching is an incredibly complex act. And as research reveals more insight into the relationship between emotions and learning, it can seem like we keep discovering things that we need to *stop* doing and an avalanche of things we need to *start* doing. We have placed dozens of ideas and research into the context of Concept-Based Curriculum and Instruction throughout this book to aid teachers in putting the puzzle pieces together. But we adults have to ensure we have a growth mindset and use well-being strategies to keep up with the pace of teaching these days!

It can help to remind ourselves that there is no such thing as a perfect teacher, and there is no single way to approach the art and science of teaching. The most important thing is to be kind, encouraging, and positive with our students. A love of learning always flows from caring and enthusiastic teachers.

Chapter Review

-   How does conceptual learning naturally promote curiosity?
-   How does the conceptual inquiry cycle foster social and emotional learning?
-   Why shouldn't we use rewards and punishments for conceptual teaching, and what should we do instead?
-   What are specific ways we can help students have agency over their lives and discover their passions?

Conclusion: Imagine What School Could Be…

The introduction to this book explains the need for Concept-Based Curriculum and Instruction in the era of innovation. But we require a particular type of innovation, the kind that makes the world a better place. This generation of young people needs to solve problems with a level of complexity and magnitude rarely seen over the course of human history.

With mounting problems including pollution and contamination of the environment, lack of access to resources for a growing number of people, changing weather patterns and ecosystems, the rise and spread of international terrorism, a polarized populace, global poverty, rapid urbanization, and large-scale migration, the question for our generation of teachers is "How do we prepare young people to tackle problems we currently don't know how to solve?"

> The question for our generation of teachers is "How do we prepare young people to tackle problems we currently don't know how to solve?"

Consider these facts from *The Necessary Revolution* (Senge, 2010):

- More than a third of the world's forests have disappeared in the past 50 years.
- Many diseases are far more prevalent due to toxins in products like food and children's toys.
- 500 million chronically underemployed people live in slums, and this figure is increasing by 50 million each year.

And these from *Creating Innovators* (Wagner, 2015):

- Senior business executives say the greatest innovations of the 21st century will be those that help to address human needs more than those that create the most profit.
- Young people are deeply worried about the future of the planet and want to make a difference more than make money.

Now, put those facts next to these (National Center for Education Statistics, n.d.a., n.d.b.):

- 30 percent of U.S. students drop out of high school.
- 54 percent of students who start college do not complete it.

Meanwhile,

- The most popular word students selected to describe how they usually feel in school was *bored* (Lyons, 2004).

Businesses want creativity and ideas that address human needs. Today's young people want to do something meaningful, now. Meanwhile students are bored and opting out of school in droves.

> Picture a school organized around real-world problems that require the flexible application of each subject's concepts with an eye toward identifying and developing students' passions.

More than ever, students need to transfer their learning to real-world, highly dissimilar situations. What we know about dissimilar transfer is that it requires an abstraction to the conceptual level, deeply grounded in a knowledge base. Concept-Based Curriculum and Instruction is a major component in how we do it. We can and should start with low-road, academic transfer of learning, but quickly move across the spectrum toward high-road, real-world transfer of learning.

What would schools look like if we were developing students as collaborative innovators ready to tackle the world's most complex challenges? Picture a school organized around real-world problems that require the flexible application of each subject's concepts with an eye toward identifying and developing students' passions.

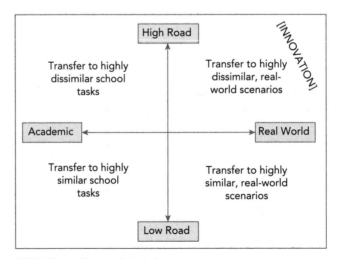

© 2016 Stern, Ferraro, & Mohnkern

Students would engage in a variety of experiences that ask them to contribute to building a healthy, sustainable, and just world.

The students in this world-changing school are probably not sitting in desks in rows learning in 50-minute blocks of time, are they? Imagine students choosing an environmental or health situation to address while they explore concepts of science and mathematics—for example, renewable energy solutions for a major company or reducing infant mortality in a developing nation.

Picture a fifth grader who has identified animals as one of her passions. She has chosen to work on the problem of endangered species and make recommendations for improving the situation. Monday morning starts off with a Skype conference call with an NGO in Brazil that will share some important information about deforestation of the Amazon.

After she finishes the call, the student and her team write down action steps and divide the tasks based on each member's interest and expertise. They have two weeks until the next call, and before then they have two scheduled team meetings and a full-day lab session to work on this project with an expert and the teacher who is mentoring the group. This project is called the Innovation Challenge.

At the end of the year, the student's team will present its work to a group of experts who will evaluate the students' technical skills, application of conceptual understanding, ability to think critically, and collaboration skills. If the work measures up to the standards for a particular area, they'll receive a badge denoting their skills in that area.

This student has been deepening her understanding of concepts such as ecosystems, cycles, reproduction, energy, change, organisms, and habitats since kindergarten. She started the school rainwater collection program when she was in the second grade, and she has always had a passion for nature and living things. She spent last summer rebuilding and preserving habitats through a program at a national park. She has already transferred her understanding of habitat loss to several situations as she analyzed the effect of the BP oil spill in the Gulf of Mexico in third grade and the introduction of nonnative species in the Everglades in fourth grade. She feels prepared for the Innovation Challenge, as all of her learning experiences have led her to this level of thinking and application.

In addition to the Innovation Challenge project and individualized course, she also participates in five courses that all fifth graders take: *Thinking Like a Mathematician, Thinking Like a Historian, Thinking Like an Engineer, Thinking Like a Journalist,* and *Collaboration & Problem Solving.* For each of these courses, teachers design learning experiences that help her hone her disciplinary thinking, deepen her conceptual understanding of the discipline, and learn key factual information. Each week she applies what she is learning in one of these courses to real-world problems that her peers have chosen as their Innovation Challenge. During these disciplinary thinking labs, a team presents a problem they are facing as part of their Innovation Challenge to the students in the class. The students are charged with using the conceptual understanding and thinking of the discipline to help the team better understand the issues, test a possible idea, or develop a solution. A group of teachers act as coaches who help structure the learning and provide feedback during these labs.

The last element of this student's weekly schedule is coaching a disciplinary thinking lab for third graders. This helps her to strengthen her thinking in an area of her choice, creates community in the school, and gives the adult teachers more time to plan rich learning experiences for students and provide effective feedback.

As she thinks about what lies ahead for the week after her Monday morning call, she is excited. She knows the work she is doing is tapping into her passions and purpose. It is also intellectually challenging—she is constantly uncovering and applying conceptual understanding, evaluating her own thinking using intellectual standards, and applying that thinking to the real world. She believes that her efforts in school will truly change the world—and the great thing is that they will.

Kindergarteners begin the process of cultivating passions through experiences designed to enhance self-awareness and are exposed to a wide variety of opportunities and explorations. They harness technology to learn about faraway places and partner with schools across the globe for video calls and exchanges. Teachers have conceptual learning goals, but they follow student interests to allow them to explore the goals with the topics and in the order that seems the most natural to students. Kindergarten teachers observe and listen to their students, constantly trying to make their learning visible. At even a very young age, students work with older grade levels on different projects that have value beyond the school walls.

The ideas presented in this book, we hope, provide a foundation for moving toward this type of learning. You might be thinking: Where do I begin? We suggest that you first think about the areas where you are *already* implementing the principles listed in this text, because chances are there are several. The most important aspect of helping students transfer their understanding to new situations is the ability *to link conceptual ideas to specific factual content or skills*. If you haven't written Concept-Based unit plans, Chapter 1 is the place to start. And please connect with us on www.edtosavetheworld.com for more resources.

As you try out the strategies and become an expert conceptual teacher, know that you are taking a giant step toward preparing students to tackle problems that we don't yet know how to solve. Your impact can be tremendous—and it's just what the world needs now.

Bibliography

Amabile, T. (1998, September-October). How to kill creativity. *Harvard Business Review, 76*(5), 76–87.

Anchor, S. (2011). *The happiness advantage: The seven principles that fuel success and performance at work.* New York, NY: Virgin Books.

Anderson, L. W., & Krathwohl, D. R. (2001). *A taxonomy for learning, teaching, and assessing: A revision of Bloom's taxonomy of educational objectives* (1st ed., abridged). New York, NY: Pearson.

Assessment for learning: Research-based principles of assessment for learning to guide classroom practice. (2002). Retrieved from http://www.hkeaa.edu.hk/DocLibrary/SBA/HKDSE/Eng_DVD/doc/Afl_principles.pdf

Berger, R. (2003). *An ethic of excellence: Building a culture of craftsmanship with students.* Portsmouth, NH: Heinemann.

Bloom, P. (2016). *Against empathy.* London, UK: The Bodley Head.

Bowman, B. T., Donovan, M. S., & Burns, M. S. (Eds.). (2002). *Eager to learn: Educating our preschoolers.* Washington, DC: National Academies Press.

Bransford, J. (2000). *How people learn: Brain, mind, experience, and school.* Washington, DC: National Academy Press.

Brookhart, S. M. (2010). *How to assess higher-order thinking skills in your classroom.* Alexandria, VA: ASCD.

Bruner, J. S. (1977). *The process of education* (2nd ed.). Cambridge, MA: Harvard University Press.

Carber, S., & Davidson, S. (Eds.). (2010). *Taking the PYP forward.* Melton, Woodbridge, UK: John Catt Educational.

Clarke, S., Timperley, H., & Hattie, J. (2003). *Unlocking formative assessment: Practical strategies for enhancing students' learning in the primary and intermediate classroom.* Auckland, NZ: Hodder Moa Beckett.

Compassion. (n.d.). *Greater good: The science of a meaningful life.* Retrieved April 6, 2017, from http://greatergood.berkeley.edu/topic/compassion/definition

Dewdney, A. (2012). *Llama llama time to share.* New York, NY: Viking.

Donovan, S., & Bransford, J. (2005). *How students learn: History, mathematics, and science in the classroom.* Washington, DC: National Academies Press. http://dx.doi.org/10.17226/10126

Duckworth, A. (2016). *Grit: The power of passion and perseverance.* New York, NY: Scribner.

Dweck, C. S. (2006). *Mindset: The new psychology of success.* New York, NY: Random House.

Eccles, J. S., & Wigfield, A. (2002). Motivational beliefs, values, and goals. *Annual Review of Psychology, 53*(1), 109–132. doi:10.1146/annurev.psych.53.100901.135153

Eiland, D. A. (2008). *Considering race and gender in the classroom: The role of teacher perceptions in referral for special education.* Retrieved August 11, 2016, from https://books.google.com.co/books?id=Z6-b6gSq6lsC&printsec=frontcover&source=gbs_ge_summary_r&cad=0#v=onepage&q&f=false

Epstein, A. S. (2014). *The intentional teacher: Choosing the best strategies for young children's learning.* Washington, DC: National Association for the Education of Young Children.

Erickson, H. L. (2008). *Stirring the head, heart, and soul: Redefining curriculum, instruction, and concept-based learning.* Thousand Oaks, CA: Corwin.

Erickson, H. L., & Lanning, L. A. (2014). *Transitioning to concept-based curriculum and instruction: How to bring content and process together.* Thousand Oaks, CA: Corwin.

Erickson, H. L., Lanning, L. A., & French, R. (2017). *Concept-based curriculum and instruction for the thinking classroom* (2nd ed.). Thousand Oaks, CA: Corwin.

Fisher, D., Frey, N., & Hattie, J. (2016). *Visible learning for literacy, grades K–12: Implementing the practices that work best to accelerate student learning.* Thousand Oaks, CA: Corwin.

Green, J. (1998). Authentic assessment: Constructing the way forward for all students. *Education Canada, 38*(3), 8–12.

Growing success: Assessment, evaluation and reporting in Ontario's schools: Covering grades 1 to 12. (2010). Toronto, ON, Canada: Ministry of Education.

Growing success—the kindergarten addendum (2016). Toronto, ON: Ministry of Education.

Hamre, B., & Pianta, R. (2006). *Student-teacher relationships.* National Association of School Psychologists. Retrieved June 18, 2016, from http://www.pearweb.org/conferences/sixth/pdfs/NAS-CBIII-05-1001-005-hamre%20&%20Pianta%20proof.pdf

Hattie, J. (2009). *Visible learning: a synthesis of over 800 meta-analyses relating to achievement.* London, UK: Routledge.

Hattie, J. (2012). *Visible learning for teachers: Maximizing impact on learning.* London, UK: Routledge.

Hattie, J., Fisher, D., Frey, N., Gojak, L., Moore, S., & Mellman, W. (2017). *Visible learning for mathematics, grades K–12: what works best to optimize student learning.* Thousand Oaks, CA: Corwin Mathematics.

Hewitt, P. (1977). *Conceptual physics* (3rd ed.). Boston, MA: Little, Brown.

Hill, J., & Miller, K. (2014). *Classroom instruction that works with English language learners.* Alexandria, VA: ASCD.

Hough, L. (2015). *What's worth learning in school?* Retrieved from http://www.gse.harvard.edu/news/ed/15/01/whats-worth-learning-school

IBO. (2000). Making the PYP Happen. Retrieved March 05, 2017, from http://www.itari.in/categories/PYP/IBOPYP.pdf

Khorsandi, Y. (2016, October 5). *Schools are replacing detention with meditation, and it's decreasing suspensions.* http://www.newsweek.com/education-meditation-after-school-program-holistic-life-504747

Lanning, L. A. (2009). *4 powerful strategies for struggling readers, grades 3–8: Small group instruction that improves comprehension.* Thousand Oaks, CA: Corwin.

Lanning, L. A. (2013). *Designing a concept-based curriculum for English language arts: Meeting the common core with intellectual integrity, K–12.* Thousand Oaks, CA: Corwin.

Levine, M. (2014). *Teach your children well: Parenting for authentic success.* New York, NY: Harper Perennial.

Lyons, L. (2004). *Gallup youth survey* [Survey report]. Retrieved August 8, 2016, from http://www.gallup.com/poll/11893/most-teens-associate-school-boredom-fatigue.aspx

Marzano, R. J. (2004). Building background knowledge for academic achievement. Alexandria, VA: ASCD.

Marzano, R. J. (2007). *The art and science of teaching: A comprehensive framework for effective instruction.* Alexandria, VA: ASCD.

Mehta, J., & Fine, S. (2015). *The why, what, where, and how of deeper learning in American secondary schools.* Students at the Center: Deeper Learning Research Series. Boston, MA: Jobs for the Future.

National Center for Education Statistics. (n.d.a). *What are the dropout rates of high school students?* Retrieved July 31, 2016, from https://nces.ed.gov/fastfacts/display.asp? id=16

National Center for Education Statistics. (n.d.b.). *What are the graduation rates for students obtaining a bachelor's degree?* Retrieved July 31, 2016, from https://nces.ed.gov/fastfacts/display.asp? id=40

Newmann, F. M., Bryk, A. S., & Nagaoka, J. K. (2001). *Authentic intellectual work and standardized tests: Conflict or coexistence?* Consortium on Chicago School Research. Retrieved June 7, 2017, from http://files.eric.ed.gov/fulltext/ED470299.pdf

Nottingham, J. (2017). *The learning challenge: How to guide your students through the pit of learning.* Thousand Oaks, CA: Corwin.

Ontario Curriculum. (2013). Retrieved from http://www.edu.gov.on.ca/eng/curriculum/elementary/sshg18curr2013.pdf

Palmer, P. J. (2008). *The courage to teach: Exploring the inner landscape of a teacher's life.* San Francisco, CA: Jossey-Bass.

Paul, R. (n.d.). *The art of redesigning instruction.* Retrieved April 10, 2016, from http://www.criticalthinking.org/pages/the-art-of-redesigning-instruction/520

Paul, R., & Elder, L. (2013). *The thinker's guide to how to write a paragraph: The art of substantive writing.* Tomales, CA: Foundation for Critical Thinking.

Perkins, D. N., & Salomon, G. (1988). Teaching for transfer. *Educational Leadership.* Retrieved from http://www.ascd.org/ASCD/pdf/journals/ed_lead/el_198809_perkins.pdf

Perkins, D., & Salomon, G. (1992). Transfer of learning. *International Encyclopedia of Education* (2nd ed.). Oxford, UK: Pergamon Press.

Personalized learning: A working definition. (2014). Retrieved May 7, 2016, from https://assets.documentcloud.org/documents/1311874/personalized-learning-working-definition-fall2014.pdf

Pink, D. H. (2011). Drive: *The surprising truth about what motivates us.* New York, NY: Riverhead Books.

Rath, T., & Harter, J. K. (2010). *Wellbeing: The five essential elements.* New York, NY: Gallup Press.

Ritchhart, R., Church, M., & Morrison, K. (2011). *Making thinking visible: How to promote engagement, understanding, and independence for all learners.* San Francisco, CA: Jossey-Bass.

Robinson, K. (2006). Do schools kill creativity? https://www.ted.com/talks/ken_robinson_says_schools_kill_creativity/transcript?language=en

Robinson, K., & Aronica, L. (2009). *The element: How finding your passion changes everything.* London, UK: Penguin.

Robinson, K., & Aronica, L. (2013). *Finding your element: How to discover your talents and passions and transform your life.* London, UK: Penguin.

Rosenthal, R., & Jacobson, L. (2003). *Pygmalion in the classroom: Teacher expectation and pupil's intellectual development.* Carmarthen, UK: Crown House.

Senge, P. M. (2010). *The necessary revolution: How individuals and organizations are working together to create a sustainable world.* New York, NY: Doubleday.

Spiegel, A. (2012, September 17). *Teachers' expectations can influence how students perform.* Retrieved March 6, 2016, from http://www.npr.org/sections/health-shots/2012/09/18/161159263/teachers-expectations-can-influence-how-students-perform

Steele, C. (2011). *Whistling Vivaldi: And other clues to how stereotypes affect us.* New York, NY: Norton.

Stern, J., Ferraro, K., & Mohnkern, J. (2016). *Tools for teaching conceptual understanding, secondary.* Thousand Oaks, CA: Corwin.

Taylor, J. A. (1993). *Notes on an unhurried journey.* Boston, MA: G. K. Hall.

Tovani, C. (2011). *So what do they really know? Assessment that informs teaching and learning.* Portland, ME.: Stenhouse.

Vaillant, G. (2009, June 16). *Yes, I stand by my words, "happiness equals love—full stop."* Retrieved from http://positivepsychologynews.com/news/george-vaillant/200907163163

Wagner, T. (2015). *Creating innovators: The making of young people who will change the world.* New York, NY: Scribner.

Western and Northern Canadian Protocol for Collaboration in Education Assessment Team. (2006). *Rethinking classroom assessment with purpose in mind.* Winnipeg, MB, Canada: Manitoba Education, Citizenship and Youth.

What is project-based learning? (n.d.). Buck Institute for Education. Retrieved May 6, 2016, from http://bie.org/about/what_pbl

What's worth learning in school? (n.d.). Retrieved April 6, 2017, from https://www.gse.harvard.edu/news/ed/15/01/whats-worth-learning-school

Whitehurst, G. J. (2016, July 28). *Hard thinking on soft skills.* Brookings Institution. Retrieved April 6, 2017, from https://www.brookings.edu/research/hard-thinking-on-soft-skills/

Wiggins, G. P., & McTighe, J. (2005). *Understanding by design* (2nd ed.). Alexandria, VA: ASCD.

Index

Reflection, 38, 53 (figure)

Relationships, conceptual. *See* Conceptual relationships

Relationships, personal, 44–45
of students and teachers, 139–140, 142–144

Relevance, and community involvement, 123

Remembering, 140–141

Repetition, 87

Research skills, 77

Resources, in personalized learning, 113 (figure)

Reteaching, 87

Retention, 88, 140

Rewards, 158, 163, 164–165, 166 (figure)

Risk taking, loss of, 157–158

Ritchhart, R., 47, 71, 81

Robinson, K., 7, 167, 168, 169, 171

Role-play, 162

Rosenthal, R., 140, 142

Rossi, Cristina, 95

Rubrics, 131–132, 133, 135 (figure)
clarity and, 145
example, 132 (figure)
in unit plan, 20 (figure)

Salomon, G., 2, 32, 119

Scaffolding, to higher-ordered thinking, 122, 123 (figure)

Science, technology, engineering, and mathematics (STEM), 3

Science, workshop model and, 99, 99 (figure)

Scoring guide, in unit plan, 20 (figure)

SEEI (State, Elaborate, Exemplify, Illustrate), 56, 56 (figure), 74–75, 75 (figure)

See-think-wonder, 71–72

Self-assessment, 131–132, 132 (figure)
for cultivating passions, 170 (figure)

Self-awareness
ideas for building, 171 (figure)
passion and, 168, 169, 170–173, 178

Senge, P. M., 175

Short, Kathy, 92

Skill instruction, planning for, 88

Skills, key, 20 (figure), 24 (figure)

Skills practice, need for, 88

Social context, learning and, 109

Social intelligence, 159–162, 163 (figure)

Soft skills, 160

Sort, 81

Special educators, 153, 153–154 (figure)

Spiegel, A., 143

Standards, in unit plan, 20 (figure), 21 (figure)

State, Elaborate, Exemplify, Illustrate (SEEI), 56, 56 (figure), 74–75, 75 (figure)

Statements of conceptual relationship, 13, 52–53 (figure), 91, 97 (figure)
in hypotheses framework, 97 (figure)
scaffolding for, 81
in unit plan, 27–28, 28 (figure)

Steele, C., 149

STEM (science, technology, engineering, and mathematics), 3

Stern, J., 125 (figure), 126 (figure)

Stirring the Head, Heart, and Soul (Erickson), 3 (box)

Strengths, focus on, 148

Structure of Knowledge, 12 (figure), 12–15, 16, 49, 50, 51, 52 (figure), 88

Structure of Process, 16 (figure), 52 (figure), 88

Students
language used to discuss, 143, 143 (figure)
teachers' expectations of. *See* Expectations

Students, low-expectancy, 142

Student work, clarity and, 145

Subjects. *See* Disciplines

Synergistic thinking, 4, 10, 16–18, 19, 19 (figure), 32, 53 (figure)

Take a stand, 68–69, 69 (figure)

Taxonomy, Bloom's, 10–12, 11 (figure), 15, 119

Taxonomy for Learning, Teaching and Assessing, A (Anderson and Krathwohl), 2, 10

Taylor, J. A., 157

Teachers
behaviors of, 142
expectations action steps, 143–144 (figure)
expectations of, 82, 139–140, 142–144, 143–144 (figure), 151
guidance from, 41
reflection on schooling, 57–58
self-assessment for cultivating passions, 170 (figure)
self-assessment for equitable classrooms, 154, 154–155 (figure)

Teaching, conceptual, 18

Technology, 109

Think-alouds, clarity and, 145

Thinker's Guide to How to Write Paragraphs, The (Paul & Elder), 74

Thinking, higher-order, 121–122, 122 (figure), 123 (figure)

A SAGE Publishing Company

Helping educators make the greatest impact

CORWIN HAS ONE MISSION: to enhance education through intentional professional learning. We build long-term relationships with our authors, educators, clients, and associations who partner with us to develop and continuously improve the best evidence-based practices that establish and support lifelong learning.

Solutions you want. Experts you trust. Results you need.

AUTHOR CONSULTING

Author Consulting

On-site professional learning with sustainable results! Let us help you design a professional learning plan to meet the unique needs of your school or district. www.corwin.com/pd

INSTITUTES

Institutes

Corwin Institutes provide collaborative learning experiences that equip your team with tools and action plans ready for immediate implementation. www.corwin.com/institutes

ECOURSES

eCourses

Practical, flexible online professional learning designed to let you go at your own pace. www.corwin.com/ecourses

READ2EARN

Read2Earn

Did you know you can earn graduate credit for reading this book? Find out how: www.corwin.com/read2earn

Contact an account manager at (800) 831-6640 or visit **www.corwin.com** for more information.